# The Classic Outhouse Book

*a complete guide to privy design.*

*by Janet and Richard Strombeck*

*illustrations by Marlene Ekman*

*This book is dedicated to all those who made historic trips through rain and snow and the dead of night; fought flies, mosquitos and spiders and that nostalgic aroma, for a little temporary relief . . . only to find that someone had used the last page of the catalog.*

# Privy

## The Classic Outhouse Book

Published by .................. Sun Designs
Rexstrom Co., Inc.
P.O. Box 206
Delafield, WI 53018
Tel. 414-567-4255

Authors ................ Janet A. Strombeck
Richard H. Strombeck

Outhouse Designs .......... Marlene Ekman
James Klopp

Graphic & Art
Direction By .............. Marlene Ekman

Distributed by .......... Sterling Publishing

Printed in the U.S.A.      ISBN 0-912355-03-4

*We would like to express our gratitude for the help, advice and assistance in the preparation of this book to Professor Irving Korth of the University of Wisconsin, College of Natural Resources for his technical help; the Milwaukee Public Library and its' fine staff for their help in researching; St. Martin's Press for permission to use excerpts from their book "Temples of Convenience" by Lambton; and the many other people whose ideas, suggestions, stories and reference material was invaluable.*

*Reference Books*

*Scatalogic Rites of All Nations — Capt. John Bourke*
*Flushed with Pride, the Story of Thomas Crapper — Wallace Reyburn*
*Cleanliness and Godliness — Reginald Reynolds*
*Metamorphosis of Ajax — Sir John Harington*
*Temples of Convenience — Lucinda Lambton*

# TABLE OF CONTENTS

Page

1. Title page
2. Dedication
3. Credits & Acknowledgments
4. Table of Contents
5. Foreword & Introduction
6. Story
7. Prairie Schooner
8. Greenhouse Privy Interior
9. Greenhouse
10. Story
11. Governor
12. Knob Hill Playhouse Interior
13. Knob Hill
14. Story
15. Oriental
16. Shanty Privy Interior
17. Shanty
18. Story
19. Ozark
20. Can-Tina Guest House Interior
21. Can-Tina
22. Story
23. Glas Haus
24. Dew Drop Inn Tool Shed Interior
25. Dew Drop Inn
26. Story
27. Rose Garden
28. Depot Playhouse Interior
29. Depot
30. Tee Pee Interior
31. Tee Pee
32. Story
33. Viking
34. Roman Bath Sauna Interior
35. Roman Bath
36. Story
37. Pioneer
38. Chalet Playhouse Interior
39. Chalet
40. Story
41. Springfield
42. Olde Bailey School Bus Shelter Interior
43. Olde Bailey
44. Northernaire
45. Proverbial Brick House
46. Yacht Club Privy Interior
47. Yacht Club
48-49. Poem
50. Marblehead Guest House Interior
51. Marblehead
52. Bunk House Interior
53. Bunk House
54. Light House Playhouse Interior
55. Light House
56-57. Accessories
58. "Rules of the Privy"
59. Recommendations for Construction
60-63. Ozark Privy Plan
64-66. Chalet Privy Plan
67-71. Marblehead
72-74. Governor
75-78. Prairie Schooner
79-80. Pit Plan
81. Interiors
82. Sauna
83. Storage
84. Bus Shelter
85. Guest House
86. Playhouse
87. Tool Shed
88-91. Floor Plans
92. Plan Price List

## Foreword

I am sure every parent, at some time or another, maybe even daily, has received an incredulous look from their children, maybe accompanied with *"are you kidding?"* or something similiar, when their idea or actions are light years apart.

Such were the responses I heard when I advised one and all that Marlene Ekman, Jim Klopp and I had agreed upon a format for a study plan book for outhouses, and anticipated publishing it within the year. Their anguish at the thought of maybe having their friends find out that their Mother was selling outhouses was not lessened when I explained that while these were outhouse designs, they were adaptable for, and would probably be most widely used for, other purposes such as playhouses, garden and storage sheds, school bus shelters, etc.

In spite of this crisis in our childrens social development, we pressed on, talking with and interviewing everyone whom we thought might have information helpful to us, and reading everything available on the subject of privies.

This book began, innocently enough, with two outhouse designs that were to be a part of another book on structures, that we are now preparing for printing, when one of the family, Dr. Donald Strombeck, who was so taken with the idea and designs, convinced me to expand the two designs we had and create a book just on outhouses. Our illustrator, Marlene Ekman and designer Jim Klopp, quickly picked up the idea and eventually came up with what we think are 25 good solid designs, with a nice story. Thus our outhouse book was born.

There are many people we are grateful to for their contributions of anecdotes, ideas, experiences and history to our book. What we found quite interesting was a universal willingness among all the people we talked with to relate their recollections, experiences, general nostalgia and always great humor on this subject. Unfortunately, we do not have room to print all the stories, but we are saving them, and we encourage everyone to write us, relating their stories or experiences and maybe some day we will put them together in another book.

Our earlier book on gazebos brought its' own special rewards—this book was more for fun. All of us have really had a great time working on this book, developing the designs and thinking up names. If you enjoy it as much as we have, then it has all been worthwhile.

## Introduction

This book is meant to be a light-hearted Study Plan Book of Outhouses with a collection of stories, history, experiences and nostalgia about them. But it is also much more. It is also a collection of very practical, and we think attractive, small structures that can be used for a wide variety of purposes on any city, suburban, or country lot. The houses are of generally simple construction, and easy to read construction plans are available for all of them, including the *"mobile"* Prairie Schooner, from Sun Designs.

These construction blueprints include an itemized material list showing types, sizes and amounts of material needed that are common to most local lumber stores, technical instructions, general requirements for construction of a pit and its' proper location, and general conversion plans for building different designs as a garden or storage shed, playhouse, school bus shelter or sauna.

It is important for you to check your local zoning regulations before building an outhouse (for use as a Privy) —each state may have different regulations; also, the condition of the soil is of prime consideration.

The designers have come up with some intriguing ideas that are adaptable for an outhouse, a playhouse, a sauna, or even a guest house with only interior changes.

We have also given hints and suggestions for many accessories. We do not sell them however, they are only ideas. We do not sell any finished wood products—only the plans, and a poster size illustration of the Prairie Schooner. A price list is on page 92. have fun.

*Janet A. Strombeck*

**W**e normally chuckle or grimace, depending on the stories we have heard, when someone mentions a privy. We think that he or she has gone the way of the horse and buggy and that the "over the hill gang" are the only ones who have any first-hand experience with them.

According to the 1970 census, over 4½ million year-round houses in the United States do not have any or all indoor plumbing. In some states, up to 14% of the houses are in this condition. These figures, which do not include summer or vacation homes, could mean that many people are making trips to the neighbors, have painful body malfunctions, or there are millions of privies in use today. Maybe, just maybe, these privy owners, tiring of the same old scene, are ready for some classic remodeling jobs.

As far as we know, privies have been with us for at least a thousand years in recorded history, and we can assume that they were around long before that. In fact, archeological excavations reveal Sumerians used privies 4500 years before the birth of Christ. The first "sanitary engineer" might have been a man who dug a trench and strategically placed two logs to sit on. Then, anxious for comfort, he probably fitted it with a chair before too long. Then, when the neighborhood began to deteriorate as people moved within five miles of him, he was compelled to build walls around his *chair* to maintain privacy. Of course, the new neighbors were not to be outdone, so they built theirs a little fancier. As you can plainly see "keeping up with the Jones" was probably started by "keeping up with the Johns".

The privies of the ancient Jews, Egyptians, Polynesians and others were honorably regarded. One early Jewish privy was called *House of Honor* and their ancient books contain detailed instructions regarding the disposal of sewage. Two recorded Egyptian names are *The House of the Morning* and *Cabinet of the Morning*. The Maori, as well as Assyrians and Hottentots, had privy gods. In Ancient Maori ceremonies, the latrine was a sacred place and their altar was to be placed near it or a tomb, another sacred area.

Most of the privies that were in existence in Roman times were public, and as there was no toilet paper, a sponge stick kept in water was used by one and all. Poorer people may have used a stone, or a shell, or a handful of herbs, as the wealthier used perfumed wool. Cloth, discarded paper, paper squares, ready stringed paper squares and paper rolls came later.

*Continued on page 10*

Length: Seven feet, six inches
Width: Four feet, two inches
Height: Ten feet, seven inches

hanging plants from skylight

storage

Length: *Five feet*
Width: *Four feet, six inches*
Height: *Ten feet, six inches*

The ancient Romans had beautiful and sophisticated privies and bath houses with cisterns, underground pipes and drainage systems. Some of these privies were open continuous wooden benches, so the patrons could sit and enjoy the company of the other guests. While others were partitioned to give complete privacy to the modest user as is written in a very ancient holy order:

> there was a fair large house and a most decent place adjoining
> to the west side of the Dorter (Dormitory) towards the water
> for the monks and the novices to resort unto, called the
> Privies, which was made up of two great pillars of stone that
> did bear up the whole roof thereof, and every seat and
> partition was of wainscot close on either side, very decent so
> that one of them could not see another, when they were in
> that place.

Imaginative early Roman emperors built large cisterns to store the "precious" liquid from the public privies so that it could be sold to the dyers for the emperors' personal profit. The early Romans also used the chamber pot, and depending on the social economic level of the user, they ranged from simple clay to elaborate pots of gold and silver.

*Continued on page 14*

*Length: Six feet*
*Width: Five feet*
*Height: Nine feet, nine inches*

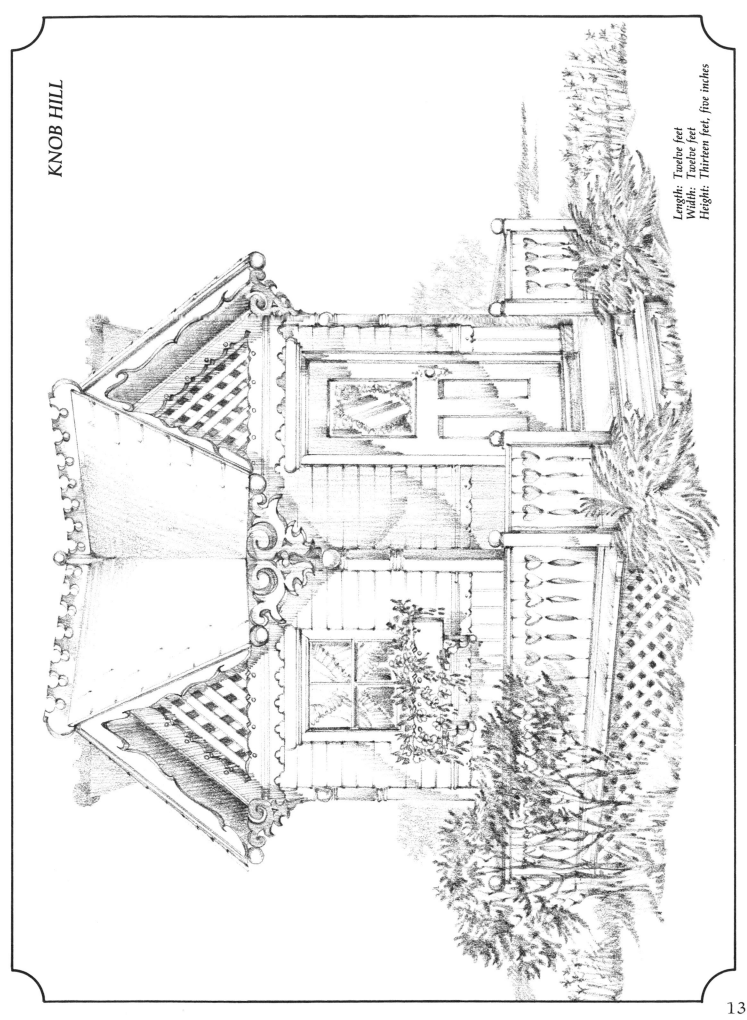

Length: *Twelve feet*
Width: *Twelve feet*
Height: *Thirteen feet, five inches*

In the days when most houses did not have privies, chamber pots would be emptied out a window onto the street below. It has been written that the pedestrians did not take kindly to this practice. (We didn't check to see if the umbrella was invented during this time.) A later practice for the emptying of these chamber pots was to retrieve them from the house and to have the contents collected by the night *soil men.* In medieval Britain, public privies were built for the local business people and tenement residents to prevent the clogging of open drains. We think these were BYOTP (Bring your own toilet paper) affairs.

Other practices existed for citizens' use. Containers were placed on street corners for pedestrian relief, and they became so popular that a tax was placed on their use. History also tells us of the tough entrepreneurs who roamed the streets with buckets and immense capes that enveloped both the customer and the pail. As you can see, pay toilets have been with us for a long time.

In medieval times, some of the privies were built into or out from an outside castle wall, so the *soil* would simply drop 30 or 40 feet into a moat or river below, or onto the ground or down a steep slope of rock where either the rain or an unfortunate *menial* cleaned everything away. These privies, or Garderobes as the castle or grander privies were generally called (not to be confused with wardrobe), were normally approached by a right angle passage, a kind of horizontal trap to keep the odors from escaping.

*Continued on page 18*

Length: Eight feet
Width: Five feet, four inches
Height: Nine feet, eight inches

SHANTY

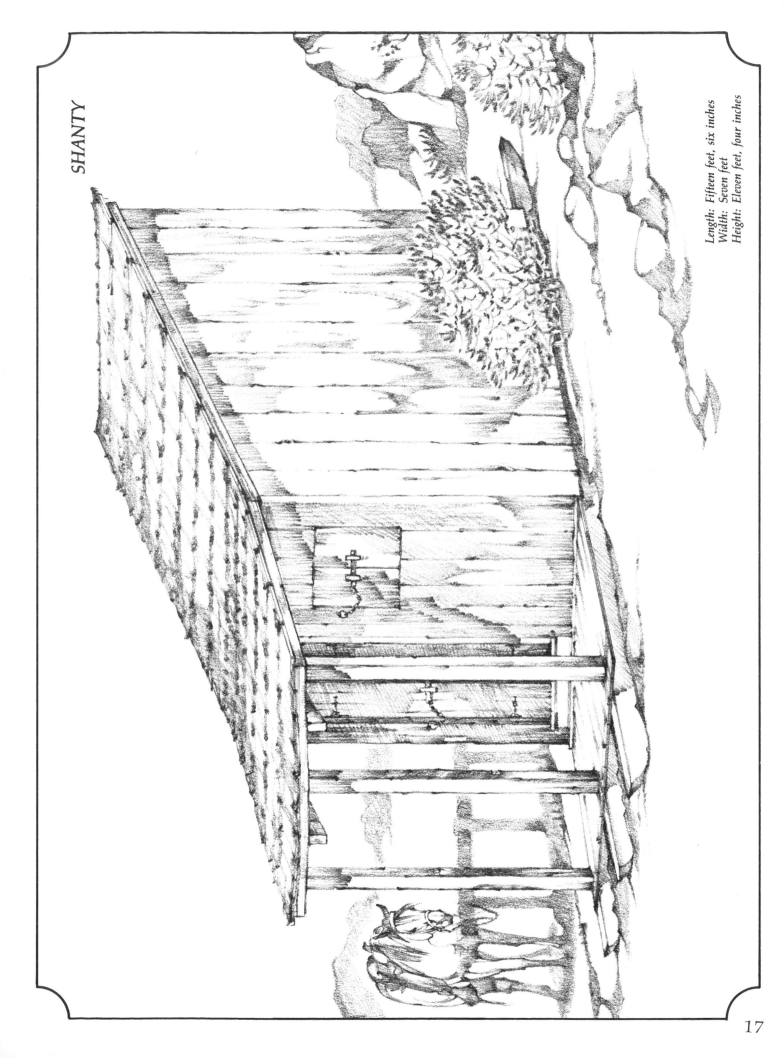

Length: Fifteen feet, six inches
Width: Seven feet
Height: Eleven feet, four inches

17

The city of London, in the year 1189, passed an act "concerning the necessary chambers" in the houses of its citizenry. Cesspits were an alternative to waste being thrown into the streets, open drains, sewers and the filthy rivers into which they flowed. Public privies were most commonly built over the rivers. It is written that in the year 1355 the River Fleet ceased to flow because it was choked with waste from overhanging privies and the three sewers that flowed into it. It had become so bad that the common council appointed scavangers to clean the streets and imposed fines on anyone who added to the dirt. Shakespeare's father was fined for both leaving refuse in the street and for failing to keep his gutters clean. The Rector of St. Bolophs had to appear before the Assize (jury or judge) of Nuisances for having allowed offensive piles of filth to accumulate around his new privy. Cesspits or septic pits were not the final answer. Their use produced new dangers and abuses such as were documented in 1347. Two neighboring men were accused of piping their *ordure* into a neighbor's cellar. This villainous act was not discovered until the poor recipient's cellar began to overflow. Needless to say, with sanitation what it was at that time, this potent, all pervading smell was such a constant household companion that if one had a cellar full of it, no one noticed. Servants got the worst of it as they lived and worked among the drains in the basement when it *wasn't* full of it. This fact was probably the main single factor in causing them to indulge in gin to the extent they did. It was common and indeed necessary to use smell thwarters, and even with them, it was not unknown for someone to keel over mid-sentence in the parlor. A typical odor mask was one-half of a pomegranate stuffed with cloves.

It would be unfair to write of all these problems without saying that concerned people were making strong attempts toward a cleaner life. Organized sanitation was slowly improving. It came to pass that the privies were cleaned by the *rakers* or *gongfermors* (Saxon, meaning to go off and cleanse). It was a miserable job even though the pay was good. One such gongfermor, known as Richard the Raker, met with a horrible death in his own privy in 1326 when he fell through the rotten planks and drowned "monstrously in his own excrement". The fate of another man in the year 1259 is equally grim. He fell into a privy pit on Saturday and out of respect for his Sabbath allowed no one to pull him out. On Sunday, as a result of the mysterious intervention of the Earl of Gloucester, he was not allowed to be rescued and by Monday, he was dead.

*Continued on page 22*

*OZARK*

*Length: Five feet*
*Width: Four feet, six inches*
*Height: Ten feet*

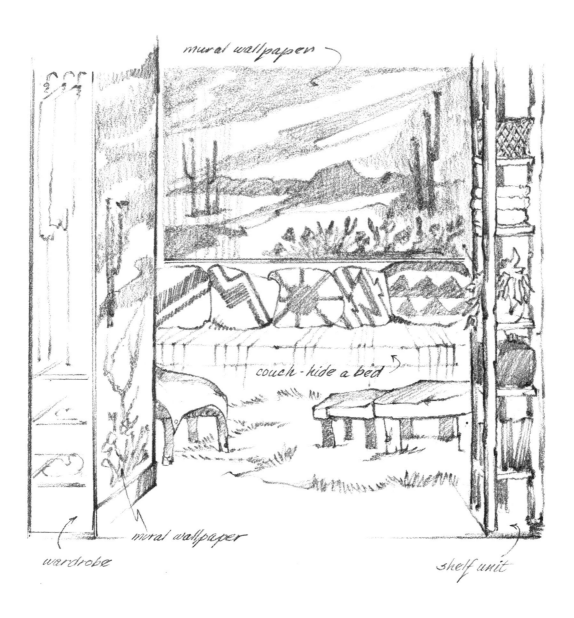

mural wallpaper

couch - hide a bed

mural wallpaper

wardrobe

shelf unit

Length: *Seven feet, eight inches*
Width: *Six feet, four inches*
Height: *Ten feet*

As of 1579, chamber pots were still the popular appliance as witnessed by the fact that in Town Street, Parish of All Hollows, only three privies were servicing the needs of 85 townsmen.

In the mid-seventeenth century, a mobile privy made its appearance in Madrid. As it was pulled through the streets, it was heralded by a crier. History does not tell us what his cry was.

It is amazing how much has been written about privies, not as a subject itself, but as referred to in history and literature. In Christopher Marlow's (1564-1593) *Edward II*, Edward was kept in the Garderobe (privy) pit at Berkeley Castle while his mother, Queen Isabella, and the nobles decided his fate. "This dungeon where they keep me is the sink wherein the filth of all the castle falls."

Privy history includes King James I of Scotland known for the Bible translation called the King James Version. He was killed while in the privy, as was King Edmund Ironside (989-1016), Henry III of France and in biblical times, Eglon, King of Moab; and, for one, Charles of Spain, the Holy Roman Emperor, it was the place of his birth. Richard III gained control of his nephew, young Edward V, then named himself King and murdered young Edward V in 1483. Historians tell us that resourceful Richard did this planning in the privy.

But history marches (or flushes) on, as they say, and in the mid-1800's new sanitary technology and engineering was applied to new public privies. Many of these were built underground in the cities with cast iron arches, railings or pergolas to mark their whereabouts; those built above ground were distinctive little buildings in their own right with finials, pillars, panels and enhancing lamps. Some of these had magnificent interiors of marble and ornate wood carvings along with ceramic water closets. Urinals had designs glazed into the ceramic, such as a bee or a bull's eye for the man to aim at and avoid splashing. Truly something every 20th century marksman or cleaning woman would like to see returned!

*Continued on page 26*

Length: *Seven feet*
Width: *Seven feet*
Height: *Ten feet, four inches*

# DEW DROP INN

Length: Eight feet
Width: Five feet, four inches
Height: Ten feet, seven inches

In spite of the new technology and sporting incentives to use these facilities, the old privies on the river continued to be a popular place to go. While the rivers were slowly being cleaned up, there still were serious problems. There is a story of Queen Victoria being shown over the river by the man charged with the regulation and management of the shores and rivers of England, and saying as she looked over the bridge, "What are all those pieces of paper floating down the river?" To which the man replied with truly great presence of mind, "Those, Ma'am, are notices that bathing is forbidden". Yet another incident involving Queen Victoria with that troubled river claims, in 1858, she and Prince Albert were forced to discontinue a boat trip on the Thames because of the stench. Because of the malodorous condition, "Parliament had to rise early" and did so frequently when there was a nice off-river breeze. So penetrating were these putrid fragrances from the river that there was debate as to whether the Parliament building itself was fit to be used as a seat of government.

As strides were being made in the public privies, very important progress was also being made in the house chamber pot. One could now buy clay chamber pots, metal chamber pots with a political opponent's picture on the inside bottom allowing one to editorialize on him in the pot. Still others played music when the cover was lifted. However, we don't know of any that had both a politician's picture *and* played music. Although, we did see one that played music when the lid was lifted and in the bottom was a large eye looking right at us. Now that's different!

But wait, progress didn't stop there. There had to be a place to put this treasure. So they were enclosed in simple pine chairs with a fold-up seat; some were in magnificent chairs with velvet, gold nails, ribbons and fringes, stuffed with down; while others were in simple pine dressers or in splendid carved dressers complete with false drawer fronts that would fold down so one could nonchalantly sit in the dresser. Or one could put a new ceramic vessel into one of the three-piece furniture sets which featured a comfortable green felt seat in drawer No. 1 where the pot was placed. And last but not least, was a leather case for your bucket. This was certainly a must for every traveler yearning for the comforts of home. Unfortunately, progress remained slow and the bucket still went out the window most of the time on the same hapless soul below.

*Continued on page 32*

ROSE GARDEN

*Length:  Ten feet, eight inches*
*Width:  Ten feet, eight inches*
*Height:  Fourteen feet, four inches*

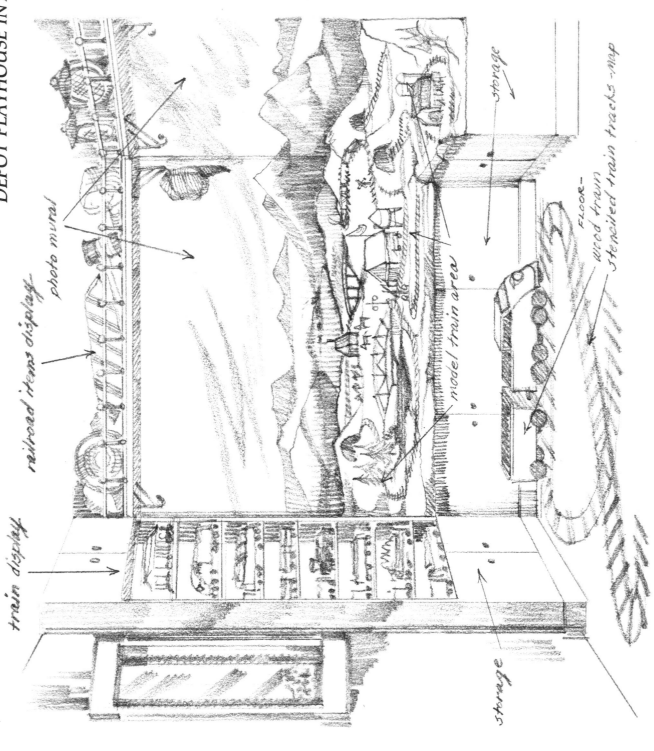

train display

railroad items display

photo mural

model train area

storage

storage

FLOOR—
wood train
stenciled train tracks - map

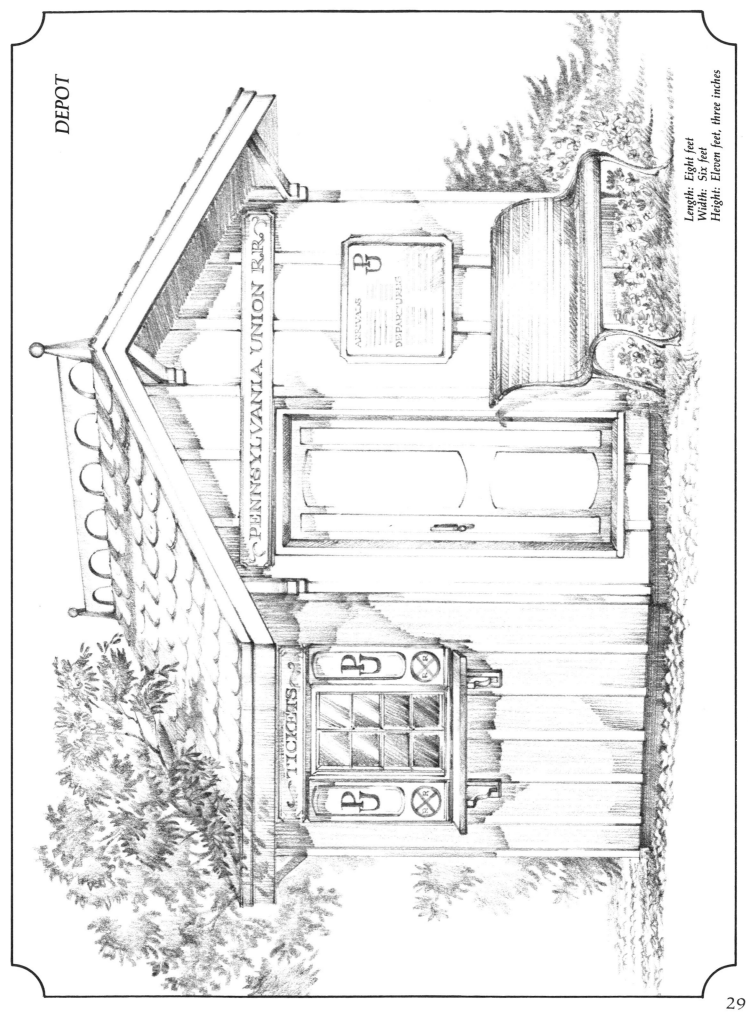

DEPOT

Length: *Eight feet*
Width: *Six feet*
Height: *Eleven feet, three inches*

PENNSYLVANIA UNION R.R.

TICKETS

ARRIVALS

DEPARTURES

One more item worthy of note before we move on. The "in" thing for the quality folk were privy seats of walnut, cedar or mahogany. Cedar was preferred and very expensive; its' subtly aromatic quality required no varnishing and had the distinct advantage of being warm. Servants, of course, had pine.

Most people have heard the privy or bathroom referred to as the reading room. Well, reading in the privy goes back a long ways. Noted earlier, neighbors would visit and share the news while using the Roman facilities. It appears that when the printed word came along, people brought it along with them to the privy, not only to keep abreast of current events but also as continuing education. Such was the purpose, in the 1700's, of an English lord's friend who wrote of buying all the books by the Latin poets and gradually working his way through them by tearing off several pages, reading them, using them further and sending them to the depths below. He recommended it highly to everyone by saying, "It will make any book which you shall read in this manner very present to your mind". Latin poets were also a much nicer *finish* than sponge sticks and rocks.

American privies have to be considered almost current history when compared with European ones. Our images of the old wooden, rural two-seater that always leaned in some direction (why, I do not know, unless from being kicked over every Halloween) was due to the economics of the time. American privies were the only ones with a moon or star above the door. We have been told the moon meant it was for the ladies and a star would be for the gents. That way, anyone could stay out of trouble even if unable to read.

*Continued on page 36*

*Length: Seven feet*
*Width: Five feet, eight inches*
*Height: Nine feet*

Length: *Eight feet*
Width: *Eight feet*
Height: *Ten feet, eight inches*

Our history has been one of westward expansion ever since the first settlers landed on our shores. These discoverers, adventurers and pioneers moving westward used any bush or tree of convenience until settled. Then, the privy became a necessity again and they were built with whatever materials were available to them—logs, sod, stone, adobe, wood. Undoubtedly, these early immigrants brought their customs with them and incorporated them as much as possible into their privy decoration, design and use.

On a recent trip to Europe, the rural privies we saw were basically the same as those in America. The use of privies in Asia can be different. We saw pictures of a privy that is on a pond, reached by bridge, where the *soil* drops directly into the water and is quickly eaten by the carp. We were told that the water literally "boils" with action by fish so eager for the waste. Eventually the fish are eaten by the people. In Asia, waste matter is taken from public and private privies for use on the gardens. Dung merchants in China did a brisk trade exchanging their product for herbs and wood from farmers and at the same time provided a valuable service by keeping the cities clean with their pick-ups. There is a story that is written, we don't know if it is true, about an early chemical fertilizer salesman in China who was being chastised by his company via cable about his poor sales record. Finally wearying of these complaints, he cabled back about his 400,000,000 competitors.

*Continued on page 40*

Length: *Seven feet, four inches*
Width: *Six feet*
Height: *Ten feet, six inches*

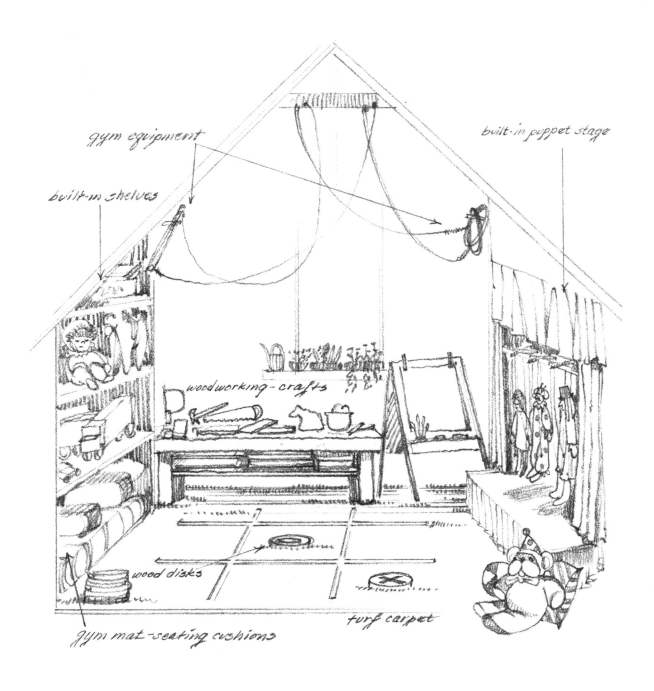

gym equipment

built-in puppet stage

built-in shelves

woodworking - crafts

wood disks

gym mat - seating cushions

turf carpet

Length: *Fourteen feet*
Width: *Six feet, eight inches*
Height: *Twelve feet, nine inches*

**P**rivies could and did vary. In early America, some privies had gun ports in case of attack. Could this be where the expression "caught with your pants down" came from? And, if you had enough money, it was not uncommon to have a large privy matching the architecture of the main house with various seat sizes to correspond to the ages or shape of the residents. We never did understand the one with the square hole. Privies were constructed in all sorts of strange places. One was cozily built in a chimney. We don't know what effect this had on the fireplace or if the chimney blew smoke rings, but surely no one had a cold seat. Multi-seat, two story privies for two story buildings were not an unfamiliar sight on the early American landscape. These were attached to the building so it was not necessary to go outside or even walk the stairs. We often wondered how they worked. We didn't find any recorded complaints from first floor residents; although, we can imagine nervous moments for them. There are pictures of a 14-holer with no partitions. This must have been a genetic throw back to the early Roman privies.

The typical American privy was a two-seater of simple wooden construction, completely equipped with flies, hornets, mosquitoes and corncobs or catalogs. Normally, it was located at a "safe" but convenient distance from the main house at the end of a cinder path and behind a lilac bush; hence the expression "I am going out to smell the lilacs". This design has endured for generations with very little change. Some have self-closing seats, disinfectants, bug repellants, fancy paint or wallpaper jobs, and possibly a small whiskey barrel with a hose running to the outside for use as a urinal. But nothing has changed it from just being the "old backhouse", sometimes found in front, a place for your first cigarette and the dime novels. Oh, nostalgia . . .

*Length:* Five feet, six inches
*Width:* Four feet, six inches
*Height:* Ten feet, six inches

bulletin board

blackboard

checker board
games - storage unit

4 side seating

## OLDE BAILEY

Length: *Eight feet*
Width: *Six feet*
Height: *Ten feet, five inches*

## NORTHERNAIRE

*Length: Six feet*
*Width: Four feet, eight inches*
*Height: Ten feet, four inches*

Length: *Six feet*
Width: *Five feet, four inches*
Height: *Ten feet, nine inches*

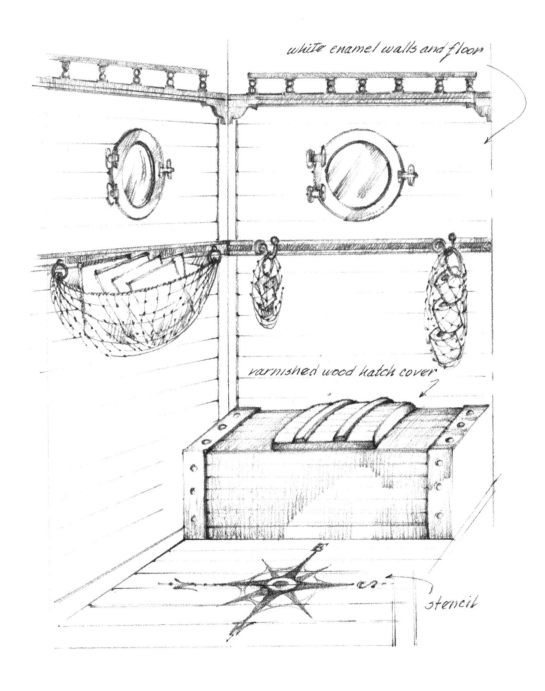

white enamel walls and floor

varnished wood hatch cover

stencil

YACHT CLUB

Length: Four feet, six inches
Width: Four feet, six inches
Height: Eleven feet

The Passing of the Old Backhouse

When memory keeps me company and moves to smiles or tears,
A weather-beaten object looms throughout the mist of years,
Behind the house and barn it stood, a half a mile or more —
And hurrying feet a path had made straight for its swinging door.

Its architecture was a type of simple classic art,
But in the tragedy of life it played a leading part,
And oft' the passing traveler drove slow and heaved a sigh,
To see the modest hired girl slip out with glances shy.

We had our posey garden that the women loved so well,
I loved it too, but better still, I loved the stronger smell,
That filled the evening breezes so full of homely cheer,
And told the night-O'er taken tramp that human life was near.

On lazy August afternoons it made a little bower,
Delightful, where my grandsire sat and whiled away an hour,
For there the summer mornings its very cares entwined,
And berry bushes reddened in the steaming soil behind.

All day fat spiders spun their webs to catch the buzzing flies
That flitted to and from the house where ma was baking pies,
And once a swarm of hornets bold had built a palace there,
And stung my unsuspecting aunt — I must not tell you where.

Then father took a flaming pole — that was a happy day,
He nearly burned the building down, but the hornets left to stay.
When summer bloom began to fade and winter to carouse,
We banked the little building with a heap of hemlock boughs.

And when the crust was on the snow and the sullen skies were gray,
In sooth the building was no place where one should wish to stay,
We did our duties promptly, there one purpose swayed our mind,
We tarried not nor lingered long on what was left behind.

The torture of that icy seat would make a Spartan sob,
For needs must scrape the gooseflesh with a lacerating cob,
That from a frost-encrusted nail was suspended by a string —
My father was a frugal man and wasted not a thing.

When grandpa had to 'go out back' and make his morning call,
We'd bundle up the dear old man with a muffler and a shawl,
I knew the hole on which he sat — 'twas padded all around,
And once I dared to sit there — 'twas all too wide I found.

My loins were all too little, and I jack-knifed there to stay,
They had to come and pry me out or I'd have passed away.
Then father said ambition was a thing that boys should shun,
And I must use the children's hole till childhood days are done.

And still I marvel at the craft that cut those holes so true;
The baby hole and the slender hole that fitted Sister Sue,
The dear old country landmark; I've tramped around a bit,
And in the lap of luxury my lot has been to sit.

But ere I die I'll eat the fruit of trees I've robbed of yore,
Then see the shanty where my name is carved upon the door,
I ween the old familiar smell will soothe my jaded soul,
I'm now a man, but none the less, I'll try the children's hole.

*Sometimes attributed to James Whitcomb Riley*

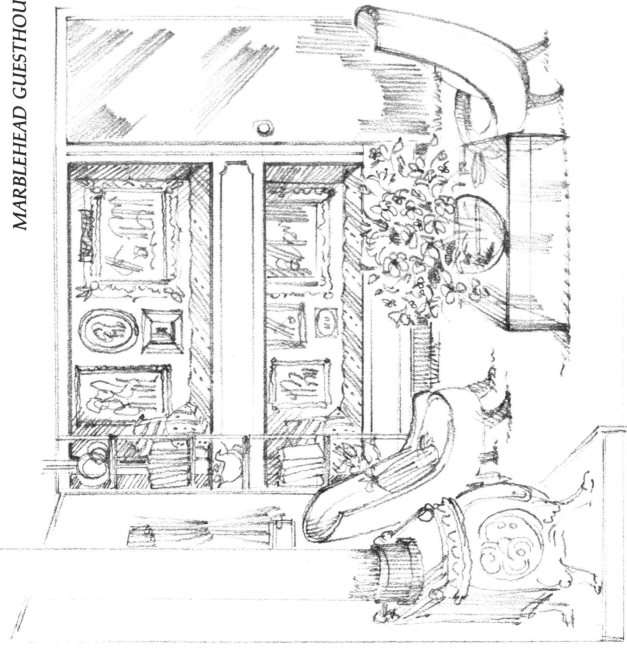

MARBLEHEAD

Length: Ten feet
Width: Ten feet
Height: Eleven feet

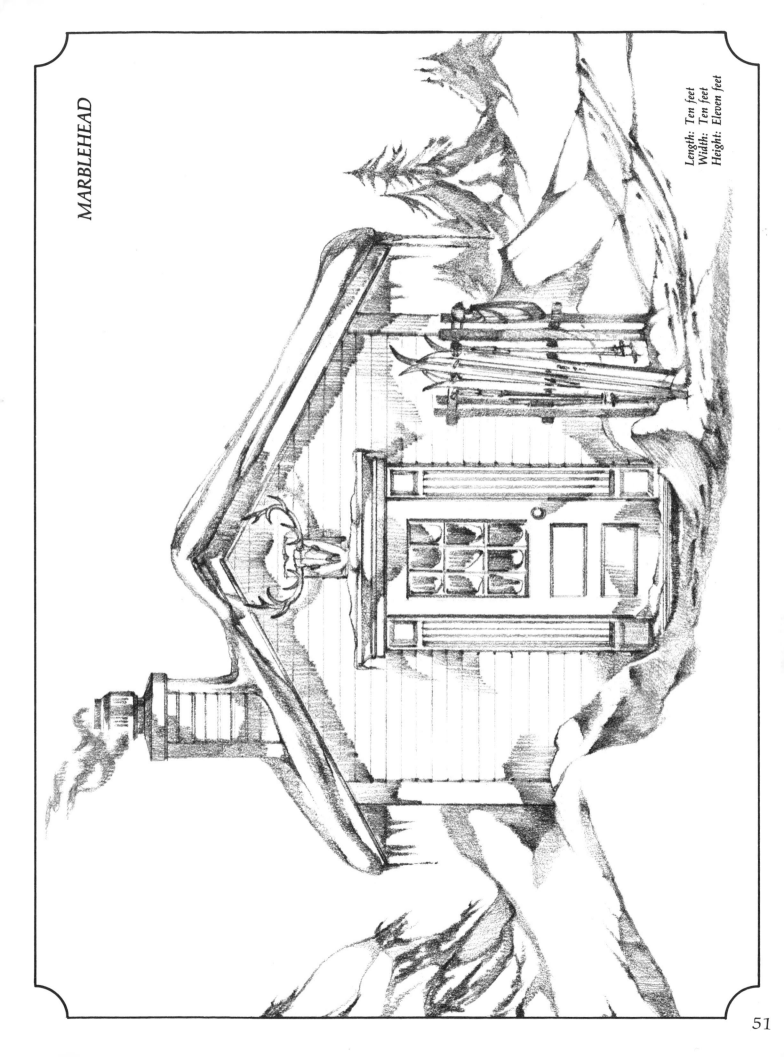

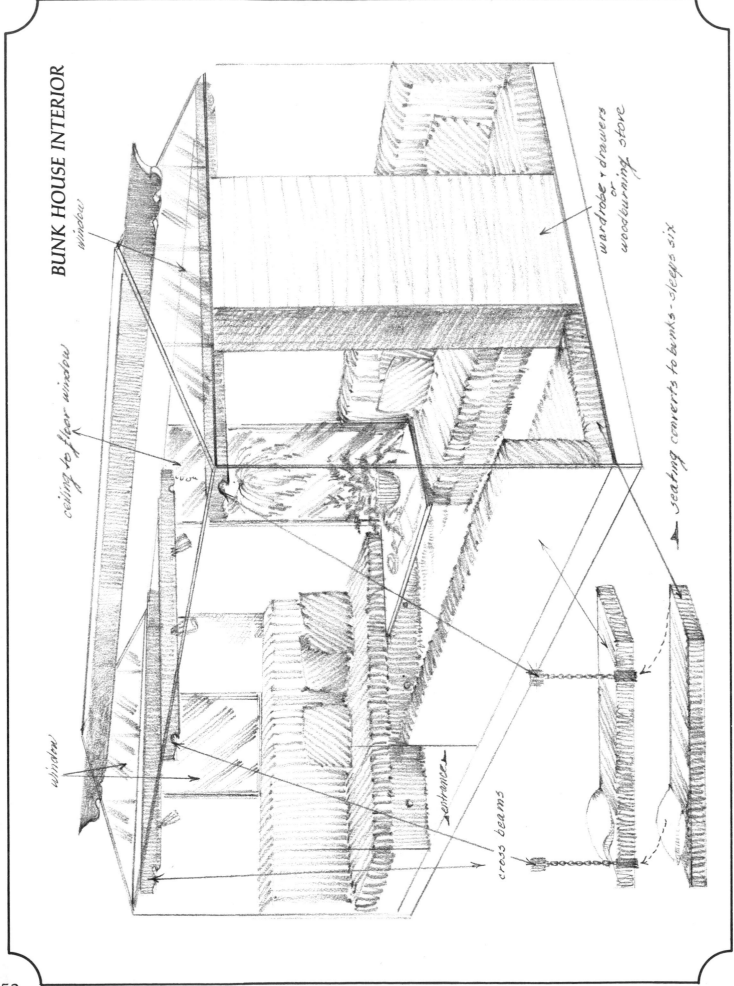

BUNK HOUSE INTERIOR

window

ceiling to floor window

window

entrance

cross beams

wardrobe & drawers
or
woodburning stove

seating converts to bunks - sleeps six

# BUNK HOUSE

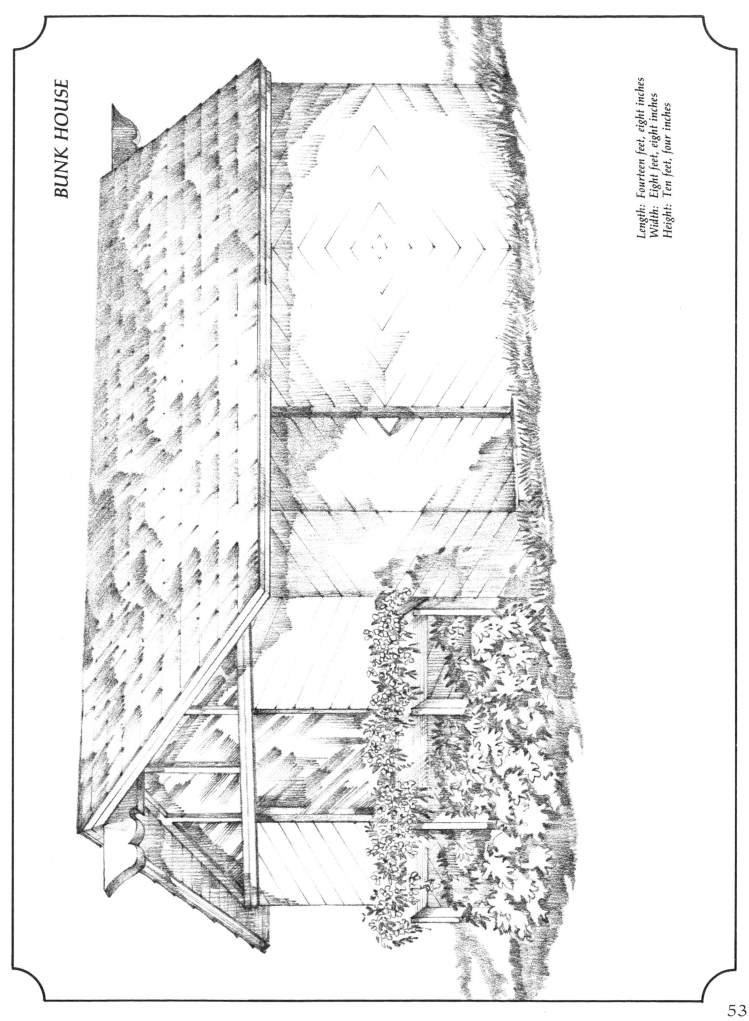

*Length: Fourteen feet, eight inches*
*Width: Eight feet, eight inches*
*Height: Ten feet, four inches*

*Length: Six feet, five inches*
*Width: Six feet, five inches*
*Height: Thirteen feet, four inches*

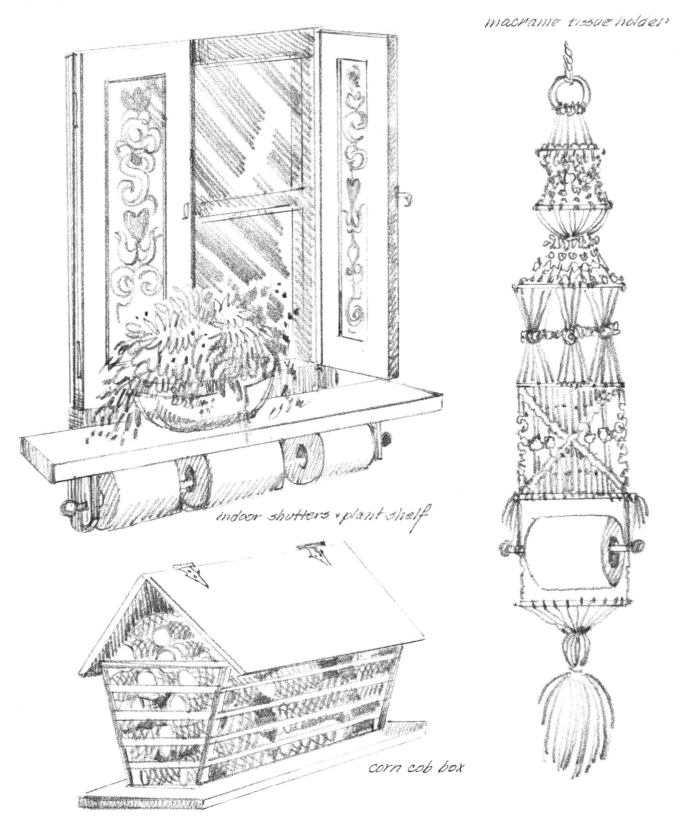

macrame tissue holder

indoor shutters • plant shelf

corn cob box

wall unit for magazines & tissue

weather vane

hanging basket

toddlers seat

baskets

rules of privy framed with toilet seat

door bell

weather vane

## RULES OF THE PRIVY

- *Parking Limit:*
*2 minutes on holidays*
*7 minutes in summer*
*12 minutes in winter*
- *Men: raise seat if not sitting.*
- *Smokers and lefthanders sit to the left.*
- *Refill catalog and corn cob box when empty.*
- *Do not comment on other occupants eating habits.*
- *Use only one seat at a time (except on New Years' Eve).*
- *Do not walk on seats.*
- *Not responsible for any newspapers or books left here.*
- *Keep your shoes on.*
- *No drinking or gambling.*
- *Don't shoot animals in privy.*
- *Please observe our four-page limit.*
- *Don't discuss your condition with other occupants.*
- *No fighting.*
- *Waiting must be done outside if full.*
- *Taco, refried beans, sauerkraut and herring eaters,*
*use neighbors privy.*
- *Knock once to determine if occupied.*
- *Knock twice for emergency, and,*
*If you hear someone running on the path, get out quickly.*

# PRIVY PLANS

## General Recommendations for Privy Construction and Design Notes

We believe these general recommendations to be good advice and should be followed when building a working Privy.

To begin with, contact should be made with your local unit of government to inquire about state and local zoning regulations regarding Privies. If there is a difference between these plans and local codes, the codes should be followed in all cases.

Privies should not be located on property lines, near streets or public thoroughfares, fences, buildings, embankments, or other structures, so as to provide ample room for the construction of a mound of at least 24" around the Privy, and sloping away from the domestic water supply. The soil removed when digging the pit can be used for mounding and should be sodded or sealed when completed to prevent erosion. Pits also should not be located less than 100 feet from any well, spring, or other source of domestic water supply. An earth Privy (pitless) should be at least 250 feet from a water source.

For proper functioning and water protection, it is essential for the privy pit to be placed in a location which will provide proper percolation of the liquid contents into the surrounding ground formation. Limestone, solid rock, tight clay formations and a high water table are several common conditions that will prevent this from happening and should be avoided.

All work should be done in a workmanlike manner and care should be taken to see that all privy parts are properly nailed, fastened and fitted. This is important in maintaining a fly-tight pit, as are covers for when the unit is not in use, and covering the vent with a fine durable screen.

Decorating can be done with the paint and colors of your choice, but it is normally good practice to keep the interior light. Curtains or blinds can be used to shut off a direct view into the Privy through windows or open doors.

Your Privy will certainly give you many years of good service if properly constructed, maintained and properly serviced. For example, after each visit the user should sprinkle (one cup) wood ashes, coal or trash ash, or agricultural quicklime into the Privy pit. Seats and lids should be cleaned weekly with soapy water or disinfectant. During the fly and mosquito season you can destroy the insect eggs with a weekly treatment of one pint of crude, fuel, or crankcase oil poured over the pit contents. A borax solution or kerosene will also work. Never put garbage into your Privy pit.

When the pit is filled to within 18" of the undersides of the floor, move the privy to a new location and fill in the old pit with clean dirt.

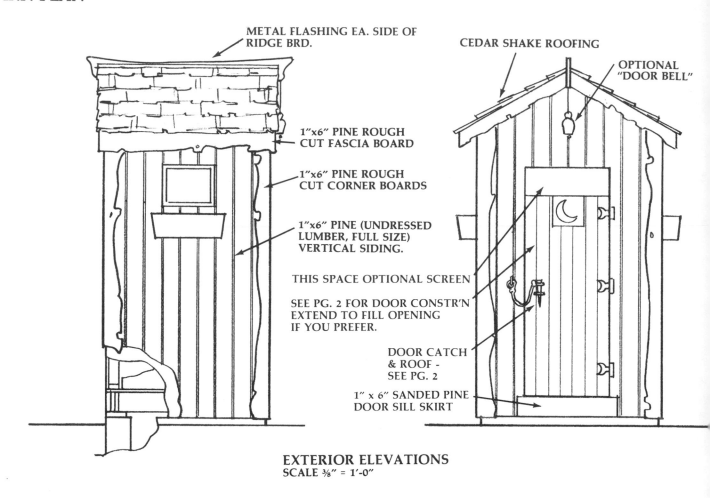

METAL FLASHING EA. SIDE OF RIDGE BRD.

CEDAR SHAKE ROOFING

OPTIONAL "DOOR BELL"

1"x6" PINE ROUGH CUT FASCIA BOARD

1"x6" PINE ROUGH CUT CORNER BOARDS

1"x6" PINE (UNDRESSED LUMBER, FULL SIZE) VERTICAL SIDING.

THIS SPACE OPTIONAL SCREEN

SEE PG. 2 FOR DOOR CONSTR'N EXTEND TO FILL OPENING IF YOU PREFER.

DOOR CATCH & ROOF - SEE PG. 2

1" x 6" SANDED PINE DOOR SILL SKIRT

**EXTERIOR ELEVATIONS**
SCALE ⅜" = 1'-0"

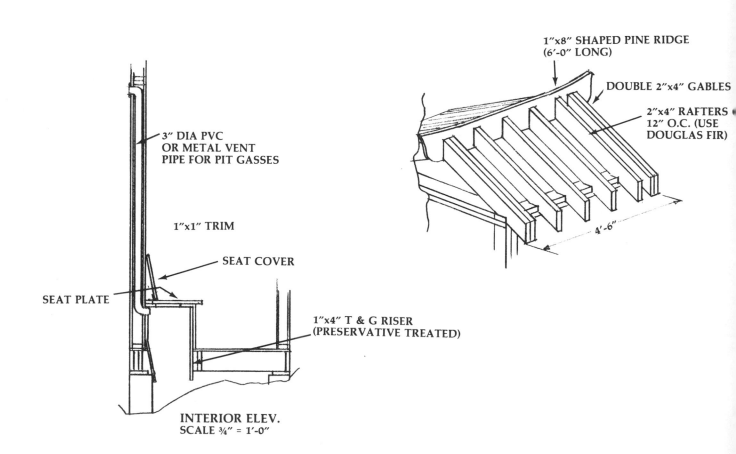

3" DIA PVC OR METAL VENT PIPE FOR PIT GASSES

1"x1" TRIM

SEAT COVER

SEAT PLATE

1"x4" T & G RISER (PRESERVATIVE TREATED)

1"x8" SHAPED PINE RIDGE (6'-0" LONG)

DOUBLE 2"x4" GABLES

2"x4" RAFTERS 12" O.C. (USE DOUGLAS FIR)

4'-6"

**INTERIOR ELEV.**
SCALE ¾" = 1'-0"

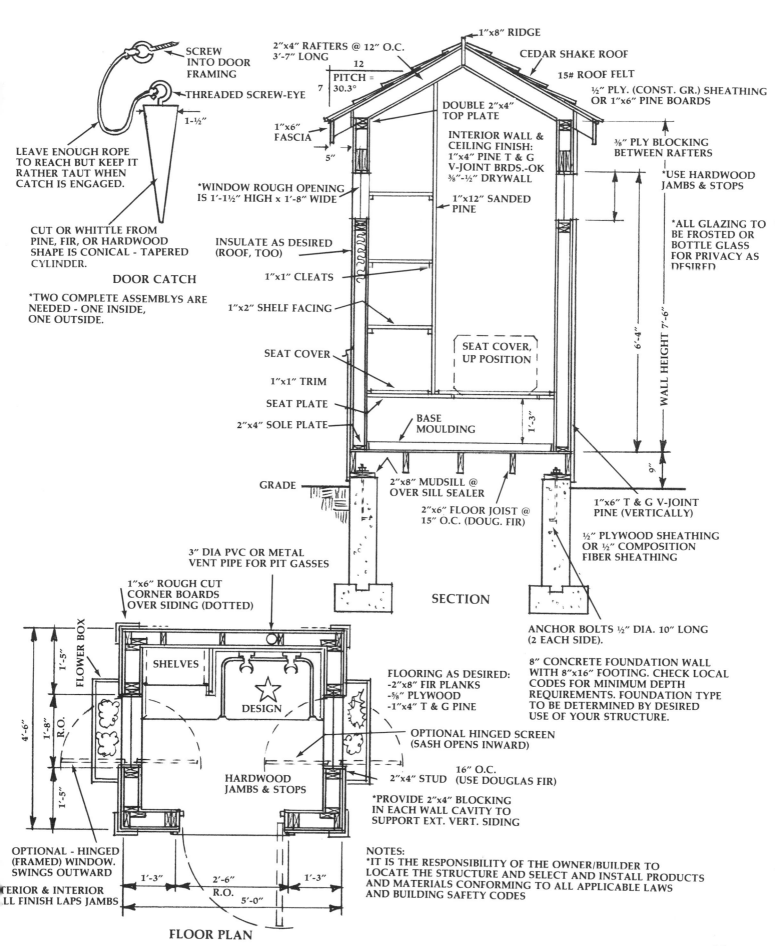

SCREW INTO DOOR FRAMING

THREADED SCREW-EYE

1-½"

LEAVE ENOUGH ROPE TO REACH BUT KEEP IT RATHER TAUT WHEN CATCH IS ENGAGED.

CUT OR WHITTLE FROM PINE, FIR, OR HARDWOOD SHAPE IS CONICAL - TAPERED CYLINDER.

**DOOR CATCH**

*TWO COMPLETE ASSEMBLYS ARE NEEDED - ONE INSIDE, ONE OUTSIDE.

2"x4" RAFTERS @ 12" O.C. 3'-7" LONG

12
PITCH = 30.3°
7

1"x8" RIDGE

CEDAR SHAKE ROOF

15# ROOF FELT

½" PLY. (CONST. GR.) SHEATHING OR 1"x6" PINE BOARDS

DOUBLE 2"x4" TOP PLATE

1"x6" FASCIA

5"

INTERIOR WALL & CEILING FINISH: 1"x4" PINE T & G V-JOINT BRDS.-OK ⅜"-½" DRYWALL

1"x12" SANDED PINE

⅜" PLY BLOCKING BETWEEN RAFTERS

*USE HARDWOOD JAMBS & STOPS

*WINDOW ROUGH OPENING IS 1'-1½" HIGH x 1'-8" WIDE

INSULATE AS DESIRED (ROOF, TOO)

1"x1" CLEATS

1"x2" SHELF FACING

SEAT COVER

1"x1" TRIM

SEAT PLATE

2"x4" SOLE PLATE

SEAT COVER, UP POSITION

*ALL GLAZING TO BE FROSTED OR BOTTLE GLASS FOR PRIVACY AS DESIRED

6'-4"

WALL HEIGHT 7'-6"

BASE MOULDING

1'-3"

GRADE

2"x8" MUDSILL @ OVER SILL SEALER

2"x6" FLOOR JOIST @ 15" O.C. (DOUG. FIR)

9"

1"x6" T & G V-JOINT PINE (VERTICALLY)

½" PLYWOOD SHEATHING OR ½" COMPOSITION FIBER SHEATHING

**SECTION**

3" DIA PVC OR METAL VENT PIPE FOR PIT GASSES

1"x6" ROUGH CUT CORNER BOARDS OVER SIDING (DOTTED)

FLOWER BOX

1'-5"

SHELVES

DESIGN

4'-6"

R.O. 1'-8"

1'-5"

OPTIONAL - HINGED (FRAMED) WINDOW. SWINGS OUTWARD

TERIOR & INTERIOR LL FINISH LAPS JAMBS

1'-3"

2'-6" R.O.

1'-3"

5'-0"

**FLOOR PLAN**

FLOORING AS DESIRED: -2"x8" FIR PLANKS -⅝" PLYWOOD -1"x4" T & G PINE

OPTIONAL HINGED SCREEN (SASH OPENS INWARD)

HARDWOOD JAMBS & STOPS

16" O.C. 2"x4" STUD (USE DOUGLAS FIR)

*PROVIDE 2"x4" BLOCKING IN EACH WALL CAVITY TO SUPPORT EXT. VERT. SIDING

ANCHOR BOLTS ½" DIA. 10" LONG (2 EACH SIDE).

8" CONCRETE FOUNDATION WALL WITH 8"x16" FOOTING. CHECK LOCAL CODES FOR MINIMUM DEPTH REQUIREMENTS. FOUNDATION TYPE TO BE DETERMINED BY DESIRED USE OF YOUR STRUCTURE.

NOTES:
*IT IS THE RESPONSIBILITY OF THE OWNER/BUILDER TO LOCATE THE STRUCTURE AND SELECT AND INSTALL PRODUCTS AND MATERIALS CONFORMING TO ALL APPLICABLE LAWS AND BUILDING SAFETY CODES

# OZARK PLAN

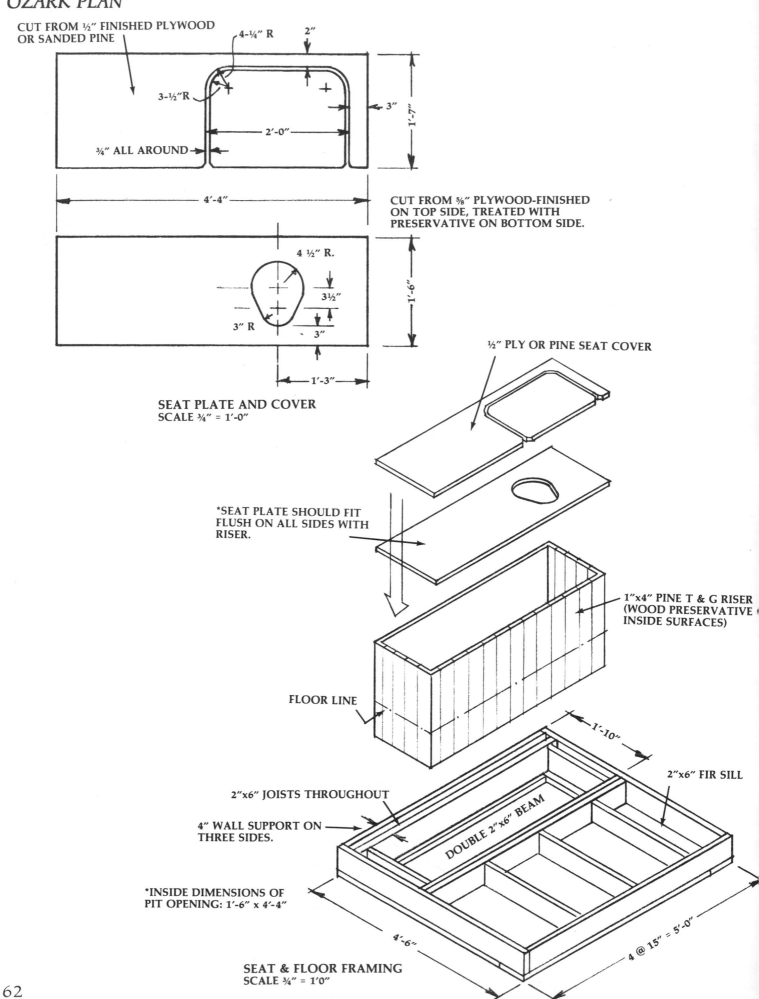

CUT FROM ½" FINISHED PLYWOOD OR SANDED PINE

4-¼" R

2"

3-½"R

3"

1'-7"

2'-0"

¾" ALL AROUND

4'-4"

CUT FROM ⅝" PLYWOOD-FINISHED ON TOP SIDE, TREATED WITH PRESERVATIVE ON BOTTOM SIDE.

4 ½" R.

3½"

3" R

3"

1'-6"

1'-3"

**SEAT PLATE AND COVER**
SCALE ¾" = 1'-0"

½" PLY OR PINE SEAT COVER

*SEAT PLATE SHOULD FIT FLUSH ON ALL SIDES WITH RISER.

1"x4" PINE T & G RISER (WOOD PRESERVATIVE INSIDE SURFACES)

FLOOR LINE

1'-10"

2"x6" FIR SILL

2"x6" JOISTS THROUGHOUT

DOUBLE 2"x6" BEAM

4" WALL SUPPORT ON THREE SIDES.

*INSIDE DIMENSIONS OF PIT OPENING: 1'-6" x 4'-4"

4'-6"

4 @ 15" = 5'-0"

**SEAT & FLOOR FRAMING**
SCALE ¾" = 1'0"

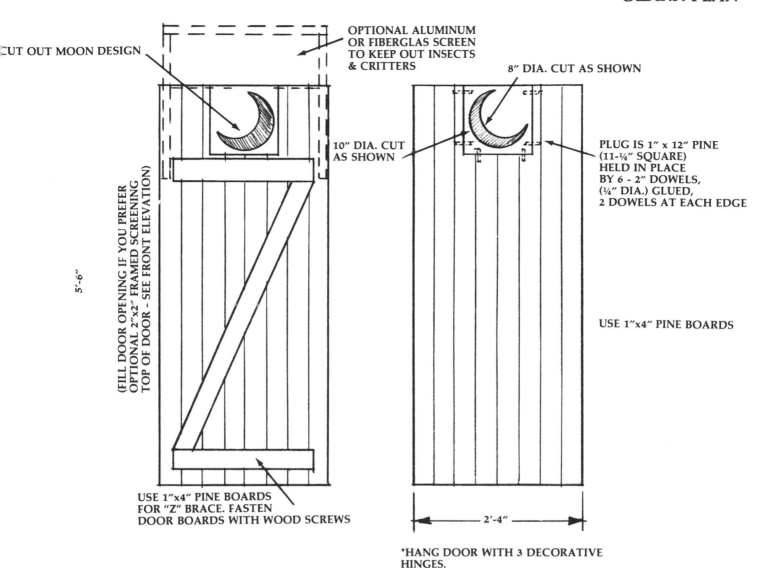

CUT OUT MOON DESIGN

OPTIONAL ALUMINUM OR FIBERGLAS SCREEN TO KEEP OUT INSECTS & CRITTERS

8" DIA. CUT AS SHOWN

10" DIA. CUT AS SHOWN

PLUG IS 1" x 12" PINE (11-¼" SQUARE) HELD IN PLACE BY 6 - 2" DOWELS, (¼" DIA.) GLUED, 2 DOWELS AT EACH EDGE

(FILL DOOR OPENING IF YOU PREFER OPTIONAL 2"x2" FRAMED SCREENING TOP OF DOOR - SEE FRONT ELEVATION)

5'-6"

USE 1"x4" PINE BOARDS

USE 1"x4" PINE BOARDS FOR "Z" BRACE. FASTEN DOOR BOARDS WITH WOOD SCREWS

2'-4"

*HANG DOOR WITH 3 DECORATIVE HINGES.

**DOOR CONSTRUCTION**
SCALE ¾" = 1'-0"

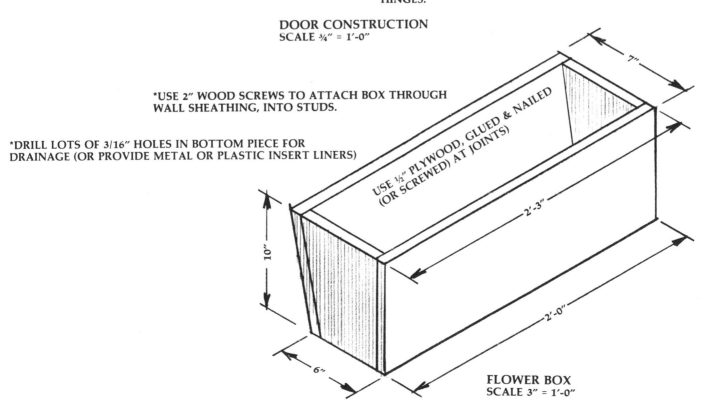

*USE 2" WOOD SCREWS TO ATTACH BOX THROUGH WALL SHEATHING, INTO STUDS.

*DRILL LOTS OF 3/16" HOLES IN BOTTOM PIECE FOR DRAINAGE (OR PROVIDE METAL OR PLASTIC INSERT LINERS)

USE ½" PLYWOOD, GLUED & NAILED (OR SCREWED) AT JOINTS)

7"

10"

2'-3"

6"

2'-0"

**FLOWER BOX**
SCALE 3" = 1'-0"

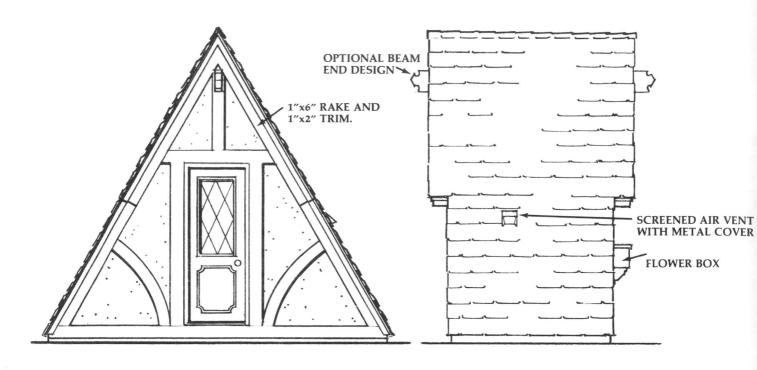

OPTIONAL BEAM
END DESIGN

1"x6" RAKE AND
1"x2" TRIM.

SCREENED AIR VENT
WITH METAL COVER

FLOWER BOX

FRONT ELEVATION

SIDE

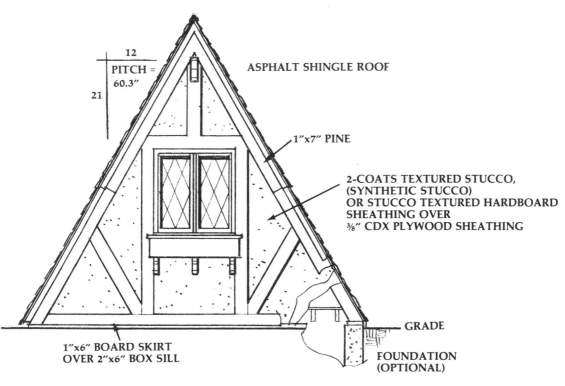

12

PITCH =
60.3"

21

ASPHALT SHINGLE ROOF

1"x7" PINE

2-COATS TEXTURED STUCCO,
(SYNTHETIC STUCCO)
OR STUCCO TEXTURED HARDBOARD
SHEATHING OVER
3/8" CDX PLYWOOD SHEATHING

GRADE

FOUNDATION
(OPTIONAL)

1"x6" BOARD SKIRT
OVER 2"x6" BOX SILL

REAR

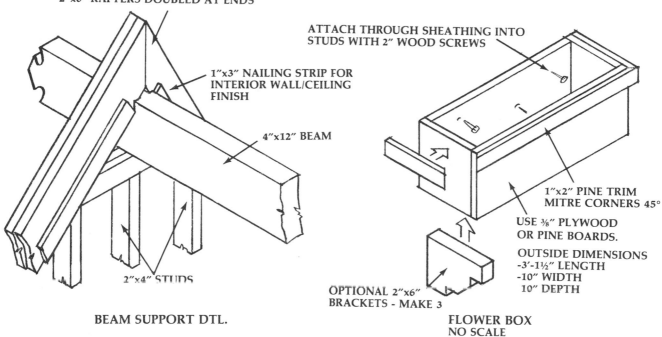

2"x6" RAFTERS DOUBLED AT ENDS

1"x3" NAILING STRIP FOR INTERIOR WALL/CEILING FINISH

4"x12" BEAM

2"x4" STUDS

**BEAM SUPPORT DTL.**

ATTACH THROUGH SHEATHING INTO STUDS WITH 2" WOOD SCREWS

1"x2" PINE TRIM MITRE CORNERS 45°

USE 3/8" PLYWOOD OR PINE BOARDS.

OUTSIDE DIMENSIONS
-3'-1½" LENGTH
-10" WIDTH
10" DEPTH

OPTIONAL 2"x6" BRACKETS - MAKE 3

**FLOWER BOX NO SCALE**

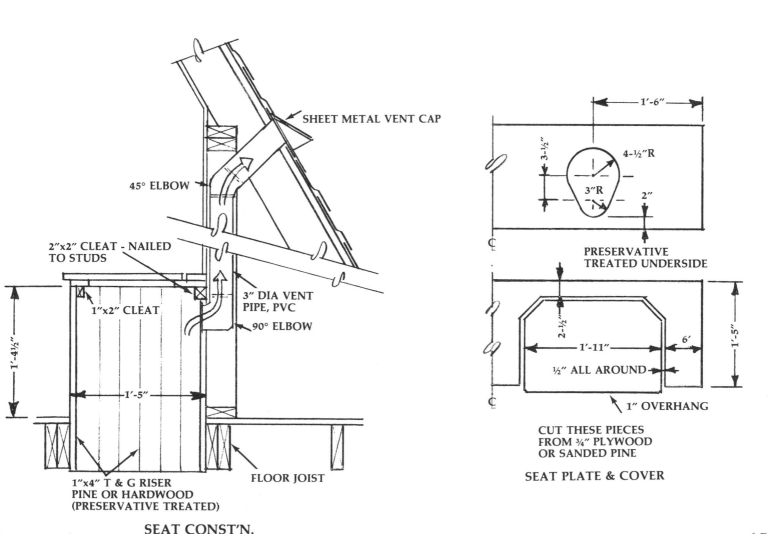

SHEET METAL VENT CAP

45° ELBOW

2"x2" CLEAT - NAILED TO STUDS

1"x2" CLEAT

3" DIA VENT PIPE, PVC

90° ELBOW

1'-4½"

1'-5"

1"x4" T & G RISER PINE OR HARDWOOD (PRESERVATIVE TREATED)

FLOOR JOIST

**SEAT CONST'N.**

1'-6"

3-½"

4-½"R

3"R

2"

PRESERVATIVE TREATED UNDERSIDE

2-½"

1'-11"

6'

½" ALL AROUND

1'-5"

1" OVERHANG

CUT THESE PIECES FROM ¾" PLYWOOD OR SANDED PINE

**SEAT PLATE & COVER**

# CHALET PLAN

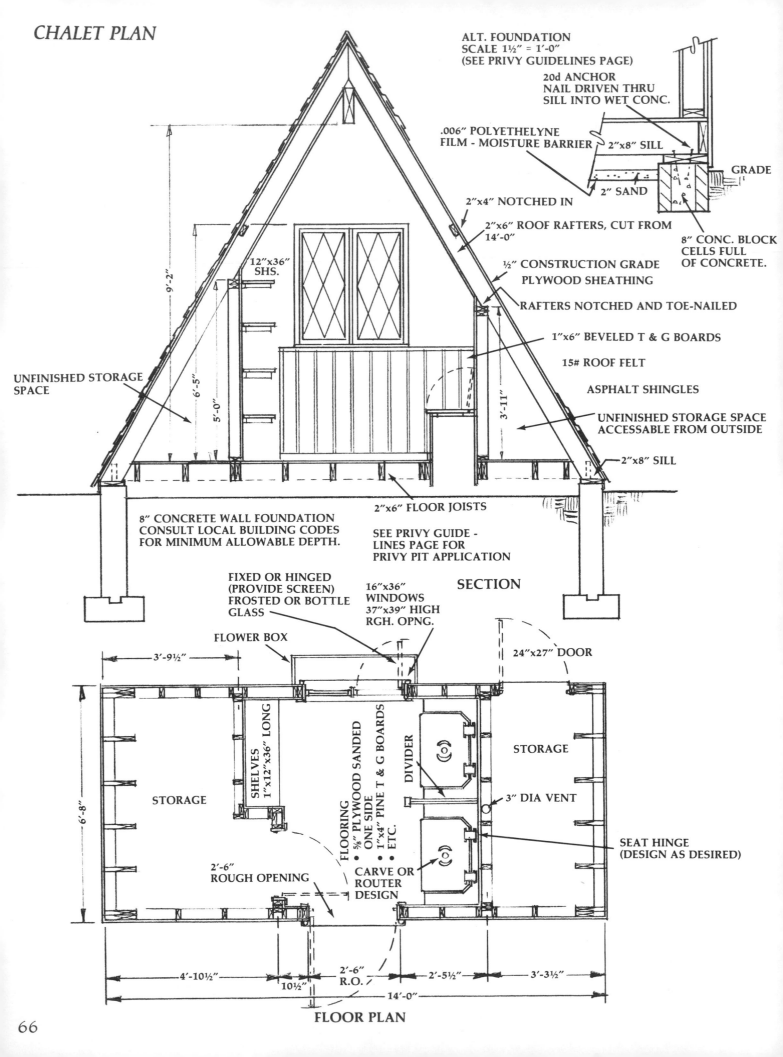

ALT. FOUNDATION
SCALE 1½" = 1'-0"
(SEE PRIVY GUIDELINES PAGE)

20d ANCHOR
NAIL DRIVEN THRU
SILL INTO WET CONC.

.006" POLYETHELYNE
FILM - MOISTURE BARRIER

2"x8" SILL

GRADE

2" SAND

8" CONC. BLOCK
CELLS FULL
OF CONCRETE.

2"x4" NOTCHED IN

2"x6" ROOF RAFTERS, CUT FROM
14'-0"

½" CONSTRUCTION GRADE
PLYWOOD SHEATHING

RAFTERS NOTCHED AND TOE-NAILED

1"x6" BEVELED T & G BOARDS

15# ROOF FELT

ASPHALT SHINGLES

UNFINISHED STORAGE SPACE
ACCESSABLE FROM OUTSIDE

2"x8" SILL

12"x36"
SHS.

9'-2"

6'-5"

5'-0"

3'-11"

UNFINISHED STORAGE
SPACE

8" CONCRETE WALL FOUNDATION
CONSULT LOCAL BUILDING CODES
FOR MINIMUM ALLOWABLE DEPTH.

2"x6" FLOOR JOISTS

SEE PRIVY GUIDE -
LINES PAGE FOR
PRIVY PIT APPLICATION

**SECTION**

FIXED OR HINGED
(PROVIDE SCREEN)
FROSTED OR BOTTLE
GLASS

16"x36"
WINDOWS
37"x39" HIGH
RGH. OPNG.

24"x27" DOOR

FLOWER BOX

3'-9½"

SHELVES
1"x12"x36" LONG

FLOORING
⅝" PLYWOOD SANDED
ONE SIDE
1"x4" PINE T & G BOARDS
• ETC.
• CARVE OR
  ROUTER
  DESIGN

DIVIDER

STORAGE

3" DIA VENT

SEAT HINGE
(DESIGN AS DESIRED)

6'-8"

STORAGE

2'-6"
ROUGH OPENING

4'-10½"

10½"

2'-6"
R.O.

2'-5½"

3'-3½"

14'-0"

**FLOOR PLAN**

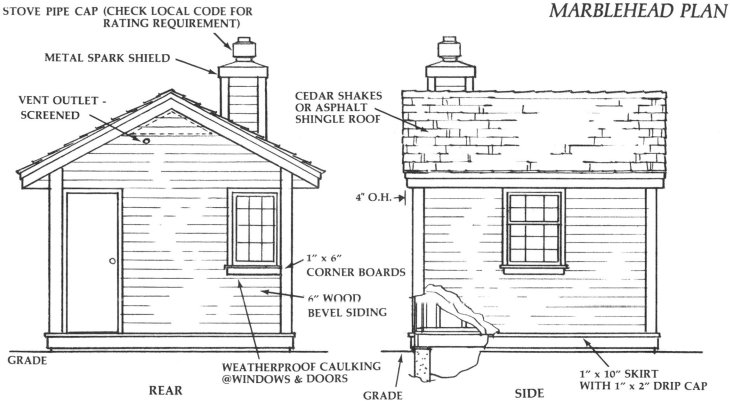

STOVE PIPE CAP (CHECK LOCAL CODE FOR RATING REQUIREMENT)

METAL SPARK SHIELD

VENT OUTLET - SCREENED

CEDAR SHAKES OR ASPHALT SHINGLE ROOF

4" O.H.

1" x 6" CORNER BOARDS

6" WOOD BEVEL SIDING

GRADE

WEATHERPROOF CAULKING @ WINDOWS & DOORS

REAR

GRADE (MAY VARY)

SIDE

1" x 10" SKIRT WITH 1" x 2" DRIP CAP

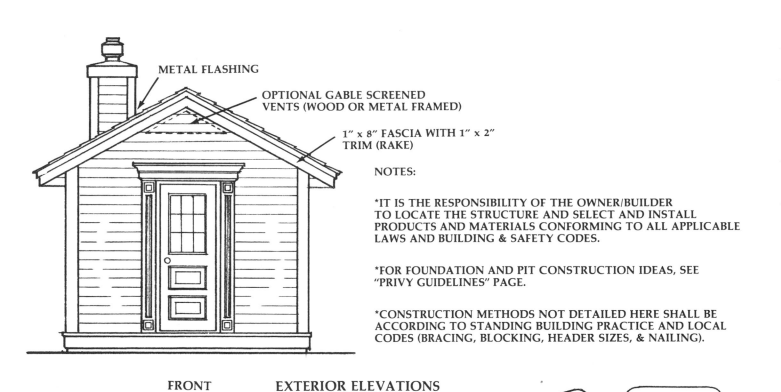

METAL FLASHING

OPTIONAL GABLE SCREENED VENTS (WOOD OR METAL FRAMED)

1" x 8" FASCIA WITH 1" x 2" TRIM (RAKE)

NOTES:

*IT IS THE RESPONSIBILITY OF THE OWNER/BUILDER TO LOCATE THE STRUCTURE AND SELECT AND INSTALL PRODUCTS AND MATERIALS CONFORMING TO ALL APPLICABLE LAWS AND BUILDING & SAFETY CODES.

*FOR FOUNDATION AND PIT CONSTRUCTION IDEAS, SEE "PRIVY GUIDELINES" PAGE.

*CONSTRUCTION METHODS NOT DETAILED HERE SHALL BE ACCORDING TO STANDING BUILDING PRACTICE AND LOCAL CODES (BRACING, BLOCKING, HEADER SIZES, & NAILING).

FRONT

**EXTERIOR ELEVATIONS**

HINGE

USE STOCK COATED METAL OR WROUGHT IRON

# MARBLEHEAD PLAN

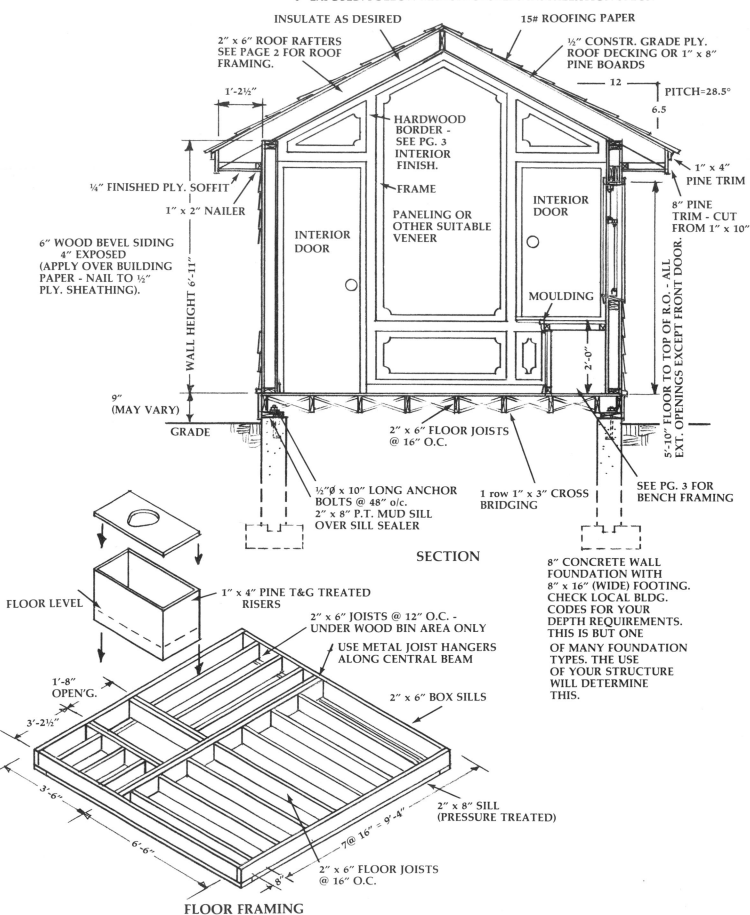

CEDAR SHAKES - (SUBSTITUTE ASPHALT SHINGLES IF YOU PREFER)
6" EXPOSED. FOLLOW MANUFACTURERS INSTALLATION SPECS.

INSULATE AS DESIRED

15# ROOFING PAPER

2" x 6" ROOF RAFTERS
SEE PAGE 2 FOR ROOF
FRAMING.

½" CONSTR. GRADE PLY.
ROOF DECKING OR 1" x 8"
PINE BOARDS

1'-2½"

12

PITCH=28.5°

6.5

HARDWOOD
BORDER -
SEE PG. 3
INTERIOR
FINISH.

1" x 4"
PINE TRIM

¼" FINISHED PLY. SOFFIT

FRAME

8" PINE
TRIM - CUT
FROM 1" x 10"

1" x 2" NAILER

INTERIOR
DOOR

PANELING OR
OTHER SUITABLE
VENEER

INTERIOR
DOOR

6" WOOD BEVEL SIDING
4" EXPOSED
(APPLY OVER BUILDING
PAPER - NAIL TO ½"
PLY. SHEATHING).

WALL HEIGHT 6'-11"

INTERIOR
DOOR

MOULDING

5'-10" FLOOR TO TOP OF R.O. - ALL
EXT. OPENINGS EXCEPT FRONT DOOR.

9"
(MAY VARY)

2'-0"

GRADE

2" x 6" FLOOR JOISTS
@ 16" O.C.

½"Ø x 10" LONG ANCHOR
BOLTS @ 48" o/c.
2" x 8" P.T. MUD SILL
OVER SILL SEALER

1 row 1" x 3" CROSS
BRIDGING

SEE PG. 3 FOR
BENCH FRAMING

## SECTION

8" CONCRETE WALL
FOUNDATION WITH
8" x 16" (WIDE) FOOTING.
CHECK LOCAL BLDG.
CODES FOR YOUR
DEPTH REQUIREMENTS.
THIS IS BUT ONE
OF MANY FOUNDATION
TYPES. THE USE
OF YOUR STRUCTURE
WILL DETERMINE
THIS.

FLOOR LEVEL

1" x 4" PINE T&G TREATED
RISERS

2" x 6" JOISTS @ 12" O.C. -
UNDER WOOD BIN AREA ONLY

USE METAL JOIST HANGERS
ALONG CENTRAL BEAM

1'-8"
OPEN'G.

2" x 6" BOX SILLS

3'-2½"

3'-6"

2" x 8" SILL
(PRESSURE TREATED)

6'-6"

7@ 16" = 9'-4"

8"

2" x 6" FLOOR JOISTS
@ 16" O.C.

## FLOOR FRAMING

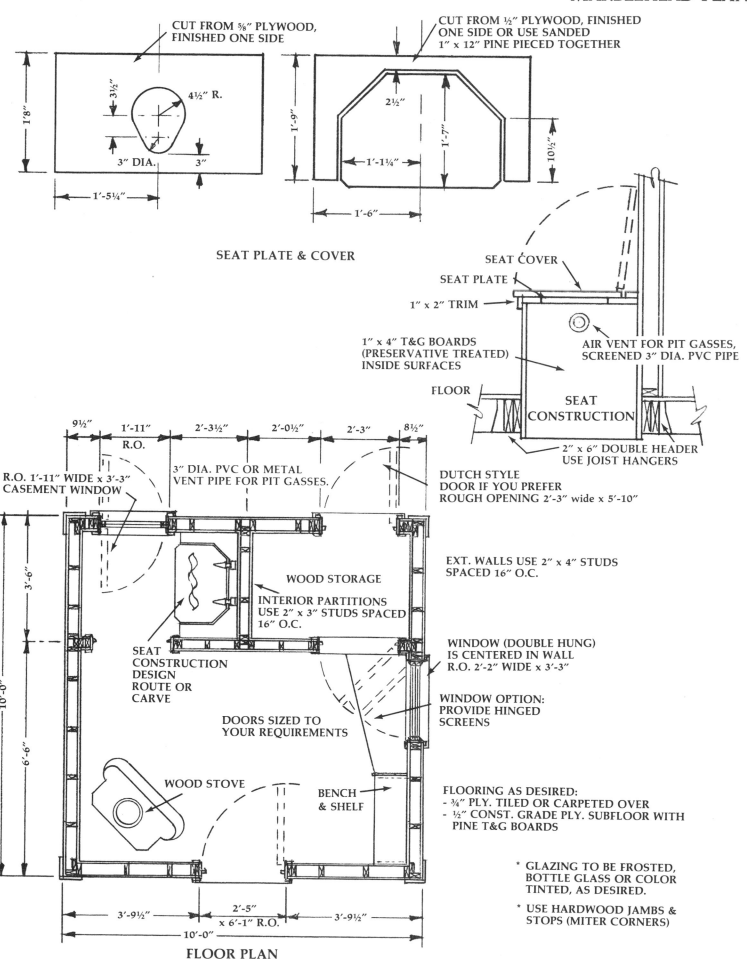

CUT FROM 5/8" PLYWOOD,
FINISHED ONE SIDE

CUT FROM 1/2" PLYWOOD, FINISHED
ONE SIDE OR USE SANDED
1" x 12" PINE PIECED TOGETHER

3 1/2"

4 1/2" R.

3" DIA.

3"

1'8"

1'-5 1/4"

2 1/2"

1'-9"

1'-7"

10 1/2"

1'-1 1/4"

1'-6"

SEAT PLATE & COVER

SEAT COVER

SEAT PLATE

1" x 2" TRIM

1" x 4" T&G BOARDS
(PRESERVATIVE TREATED)
INSIDE SURFACES

AIR VENT FOR PIT GASSES,
SCREENED 3" DIA. PVC PIPE

FLOOR

SEAT
CONSTRUCTION

2" x 6" DOUBLE HEADER
USE JOIST HANGERS

9 1/2"

1'-11"
R.O.

2'-3 1/2"

2'-0 1/2"

2'-3"

8 1/2"

R.O. 1'-11" WIDE x 3'-3"
CASEMENT WINDOW

3" DIA. PVC OR METAL
VENT PIPE FOR PIT GASSES.

DUTCH STYLE
DOOR IF YOU PREFER
ROUGH OPENING 2'-3" wide x 5'-10"

3'-6"

10'-0"

6'-6"

WOOD STORAGE

INTERIOR PARTITIONS
USE 2" x 3" STUDS SPACED
16" O.C.

SEAT
CONSTRUCTION
DESIGN
ROUTE OR
CARVE

DOORS SIZED TO
YOUR REQUIREMENTS

WOOD STOVE

BENCH
& SHELF

EXT. WALLS USE 2" x 4" STUDS
SPACED 16" O.C.

WINDOW (DOUBLE HUNG)
IS CENTERED IN WALL
R.O. 2'-2" WIDE x 3'-3"

WINDOW OPTION:
PROVIDE HINGED
SCREENS

FLOORING AS DESIRED:
- 3/4" PLY. TILED OR CARPETED OVER
- 1/2" CONST. GRADE PLY. SUBFLOOR WITH
  PINE T&G BOARDS

* GLAZING TO BE FROSTED,
  BOTTLE GLASS OR COLOR
  TINTED, AS DESIRED.

* USE HARDWOOD JAMBS &
  STOPS (MITER CORNERS)

3'-9 1/2"

2'-5"
x 6'-1" R.O.

3'-9 1/2"

10'-0"

FLOOR PLAN

# MARBLEHEAD PLAN

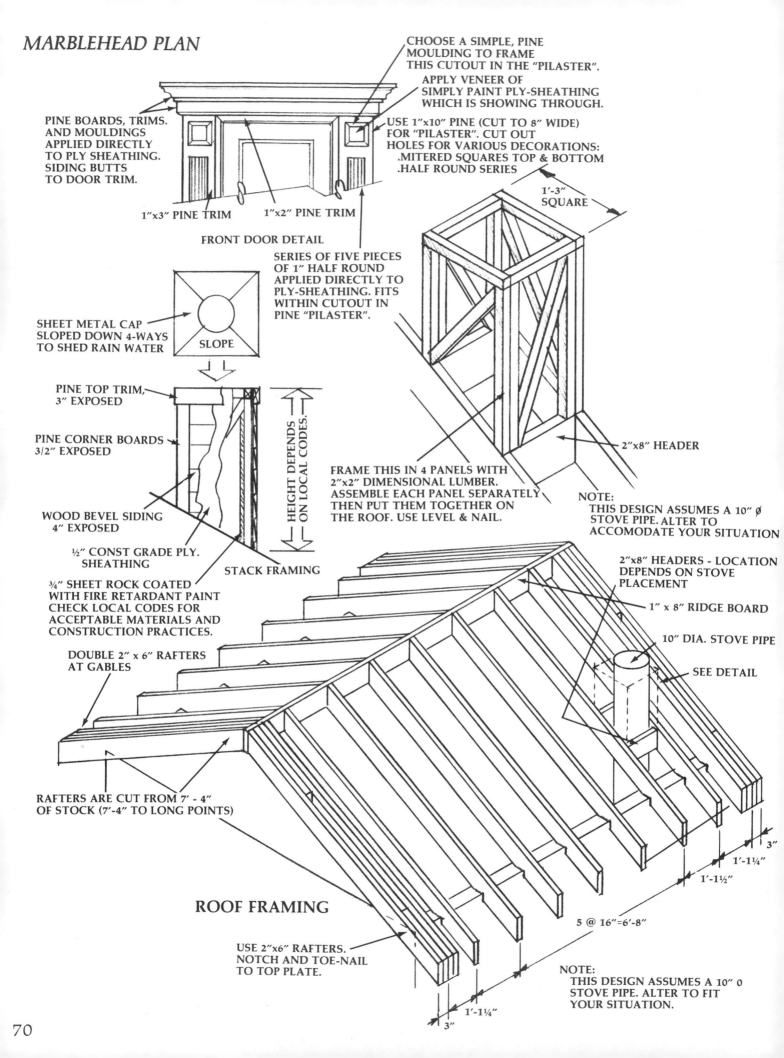

CHOOSE A SIMPLE, PINE MOULDING TO FRAME THIS CUTOUT IN THE "PILASTER". APPLY VENEER OF SIMPLY PAINT PLY-SHEATHING WHICH IS SHOWING THROUGH.

PINE BOARDS, TRIMS. AND MOULDINGS APPLIED DIRECTLY TO PLY SHEATHING. SIDING BUTTS TO DOOR TRIM.

USE 1"x10" PINE (CUT TO 8" WIDE) FOR "PILASTER". CUT OUT HOLES FOR VARIOUS DECORATIONS:
.MITERED SQUARES TOP & BOTTOM
.HALF ROUND SERIES

1"x3" PINE TRIM    1"x2" PINE TRIM

FRONT DOOR DETAIL

1'-3" SQUARE

SERIES OF FIVE PIECES OF 1" HALF ROUND APPLIED DIRECTLY TO PLY-SHEATHING. FITS WITHIN CUTOUT IN PINE "PILASTER".

SHEET METAL CAP SLOPED DOWN 4-WAYS TO SHED RAIN WATER

SLOPE

PINE TOP TRIM, 3" EXPOSED

PINE CORNER BOARDS 3/2" EXPOSED

HEIGHT DEPENDS ON LOCAL CODES.

2"x8" HEADER

WOOD BEVEL SIDING 4" EXPOSED

½" CONST GRADE PLY. SHEATHING

STACK FRAMING

FRAME THIS IN 4 PANELS WITH 2"x2" DIMENSIONAL LUMBER. ASSEMBLE EACH PANEL SEPARATELY THEN PUT THEM TOGETHER ON THE ROOF. USE LEVEL & NAIL.

¾" SHEET ROCK COATED WITH FIRE RETARDANT PAINT CHECK LOCAL CODES FOR ACCEPTABLE MATERIALS AND CONSTRUCTION PRACTICES.

NOTE: THIS DESIGN ASSUMES A 10" Ø STOVE PIPE. ALTER TO ACCOMODATE YOUR SITUATION

2"x8" HEADERS - LOCATION DEPENDS ON STOVE PLACEMENT

1" x 8" RIDGE BOARD

10" DIA. STOVE PIPE

SEE DETAIL

DOUBLE 2" x 6" RAFTERS AT GABLES

RAFTERS ARE CUT FROM 7' - 4" OF STOCK (7'-4" TO LONG POINTS)

## ROOF FRAMING

3"

1'-1¼"

1'-1½"

5 @ 16"=6'-8"

USE 2"x6" RAFTERS. NOTCH AND TOE-NAIL TO TOP PLATE.

NOTE: THIS DESIGN ASSUMES A 10" 0 STOVE PIPE. ALTER TO FIT YOUR SITUATION.

1'-1¼"

3"

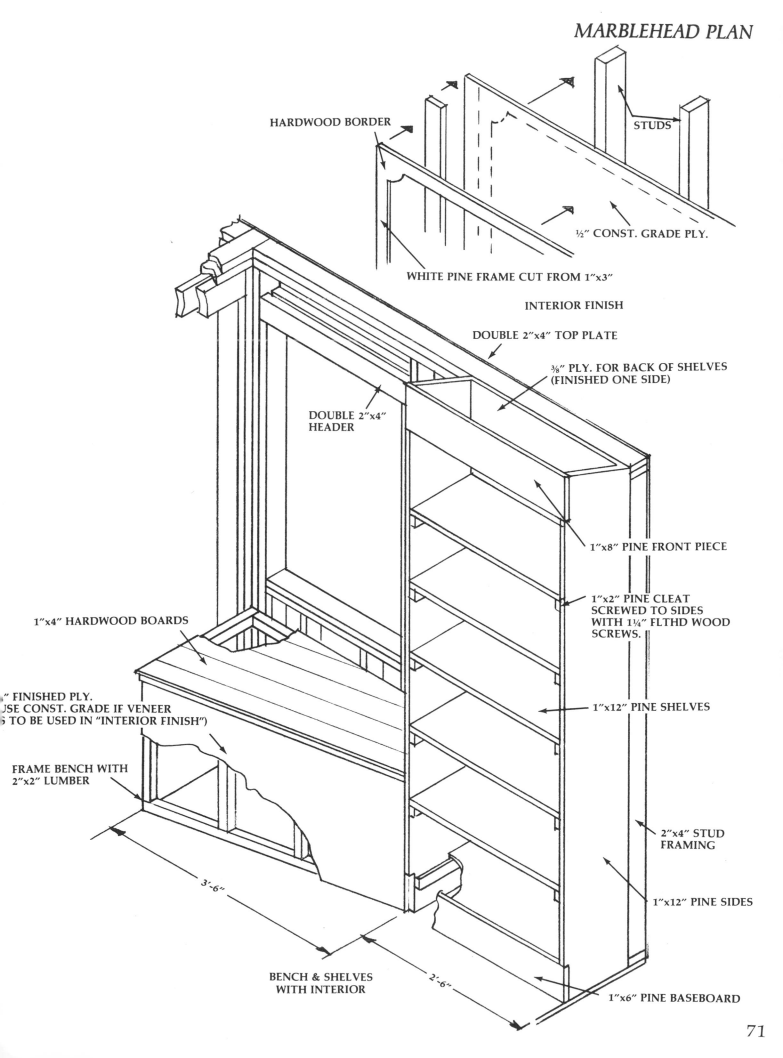

# MARBLEHEAD PLAN

HARDWOOD BORDER

STUDS

½" CONST. GRADE PLY.

WHITE PINE FRAME CUT FROM 1"x3"

INTERIOR FINISH

DOUBLE 2"x4" TOP PLATE

⅜" PLY. FOR BACK OF SHELVES
(FINISHED ONE SIDE)

DOUBLE 2"x4"
HEADER

1"x8" PINE FRONT PIECE

1"x2" PINE CLEAT
SCREWED TO SIDES
WITH 1¼" FLTHD WOOD
SCREWS.

1"x4" HARDWOOD BOARDS

1"x12" PINE SHELVES

" FINISHED PLY.
USE CONST. GRADE IF VENEER
 TO BE USED IN "INTERIOR FINISH")

FRAME BENCH WITH
2"x2" LUMBER

2"x4" STUD
FRAMING

3'-6"

1"x12" PINE SIDES

BENCH & SHELVES
WITH INTERIOR

2'-6"

1"x6" PINE BASEBOARD

71

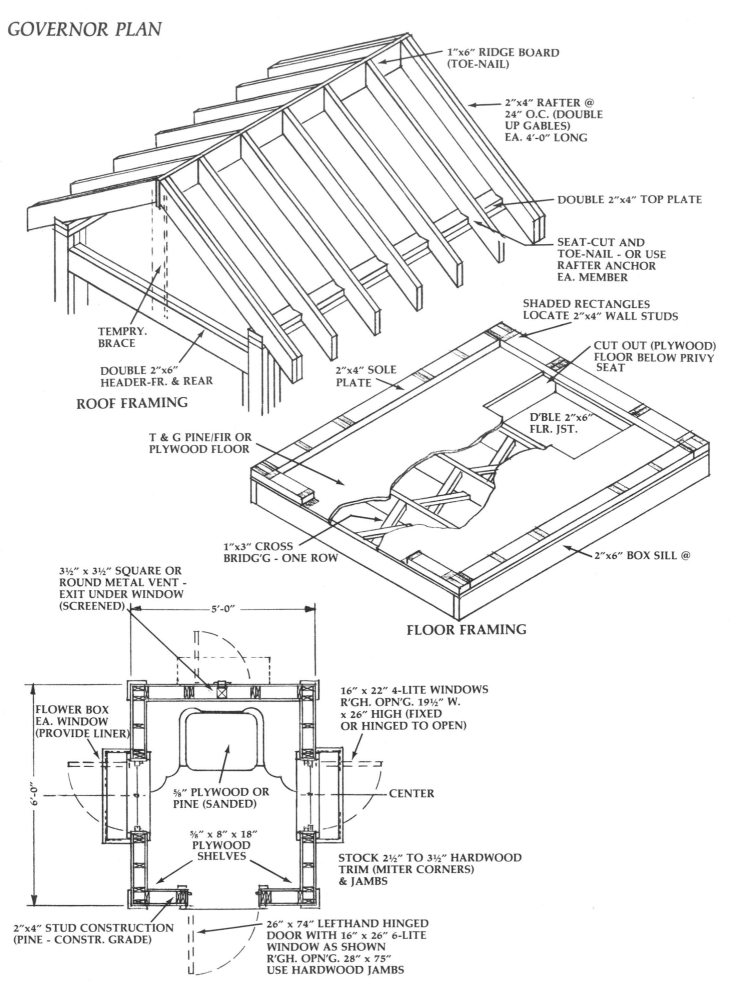

1"x6" RIDGE BOARD (TOE-NAIL)

2"x4" RAFTER @ 24" O.C. (DOUBLE UP GABLES) EA. 4'-0" LONG

DOUBLE 2"x4" TOP PLATE

SEAT-CUT AND TOE-NAIL - OR USE RAFTER ANCHOR EA. MEMBER

TEMPRY. BRACE

DOUBLE 2"x6" HEADER-FR. & REAR

ROOF FRAMING

2"x4" SOLE PLATE

T & G PINE/FIR OR PLYWOOD FLOOR

1"x3" CROSS BRIDG'G - ONE ROW

SHADED RECTANGLES LOCATE 2"x4" WALL STUDS

CUT OUT (PLYWOOD) FLOOR BELOW PRIVY SEAT

D'BLE 2"x6" FLR. JST.

2"x6" BOX SILL @

FLOOR FRAMING

3½" x 3½" SQUARE OR ROUND METAL VENT - EXIT UNDER WINDOW (SCREENED)

5'-0"

FLOWER BOX EA. WINDOW (PROVIDE LINER)

16" x 22" 4-LITE WINDOWS R'GH. OPN'G. 19½" W. x 26" HIGH (FIXED OR HINGED TO OPEN)

6'-0"

⅝" PLYWOOD OR PINE (SANDED)

CENTER

⅝" x 8" x 18" PLYWOOD SHELVES

STOCK 2½" TO 3½" HARDWOOD TRIM (MITER CORNERS) & JAMBS

2"x4" STUD CONSTRUCTION (PINE - CONSTR. GRADE)

26" x 74" LEFTHAND HINGED DOOR WITH 16" x 26" 6-LITE WINDOW AS SHOWN R'GH. OPN'G. 28" x 75" USE HARDWOOD JAMBS

FLOOR PLAN

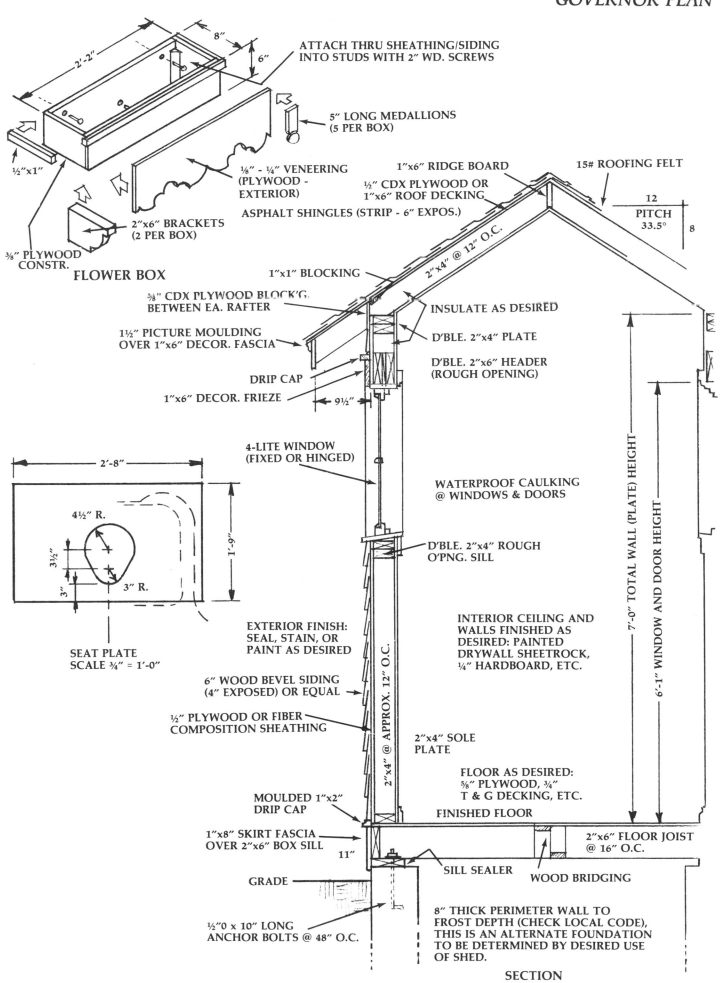

**FLOWER BOX**

2'-2"
8"
6"
½"x1"
⅜" PLYWOOD CONSTR.

ATTACH THRU SHEATHING/SIDING INTO STUDS WITH 2" WD. SCREWS

5" LONG MEDALLIONS (5 PER BOX)

⅛" - ¼" VENEERING (PLYWOOD - EXTERIOR)

2"x6" BRACKETS (2 PER BOX)

1"x6" RIDGE BOARD

½" CDX PLYWOOD OR 1"x6" ROOF DECKING

ASPHALT SHINGLES (STRIP - 6" EXPOS.)

15# ROOFING FELT

12
PITCH 33.5°
8

1"x1" BLOCKING

⅜" CDX PLYWOOD BLOCK'G. BETWEEN EA. RAFTER

2"x4" @ 12" O.C.

INSULATE AS DESIRED

1½" PICTURE MOULDING OVER 1"x6" DECOR. FASCIA

D'BLE. 2"x4" PLATE

DRIP CAP

D'BLE. 2"x6" HEADER (ROUGH OPENING)

1"x6" DECOR. FRIEZE

9½"

4-LITE WINDOW (FIXED OR HINGED)

WATERPROOF CAULKING @ WINDOWS & DOORS

SEAT PLATE SCALE ¾" = 1'-0"

2'-8"
1'-9"
4½" R.
3½"
3" R.
3"

7'-0" TOTAL WALL (PLATE) HEIGHT

6'-1" WINDOW AND DOOR HEIGHT

D'BLE. 2"x4" ROUGH O'PNG. SILL

INTERIOR CEILING AND WALLS FINISHED AS DESIRED: PAINTED DRYWALL SHEETROCK, ¼" HARDBOARD, ETC.

EXTERIOR FINISH: SEAL, STAIN, OR PAINT AS DESIRED

6" WOOD BEVEL SIDING (4" EXPOSED) OR EQUAL

½" PLYWOOD OR FIBER COMPOSITION SHEATHING

2"x4" @ APPROX. 12" O.C.

2"x4" SOLE PLATE

FLOOR AS DESIRED: ⅝" PLYWOOD, ¾" T & G DECKING, ETC.

FINISHED FLOOR

MOULDED 1"x2" DRIP CAP

1"x8" SKIRT FASCIA OVER 2"x6" BOX SILL

11"

2"x6" FLOOR JOIST @ 16" O.C.

SILL SEALER

WOOD BRIDGING

GRADE

½"Ø x 10" LONG ANCHOR BOLTS @ 48" O.C.

8" THICK PERIMETER WALL TO FROST DEPTH (CHECK LOCAL CODE), THIS IS AN ALTERNATE FOUNDATION TO BE DETERMINED BY DESIRED USE OF SHED.

**SECTION**

73

# GOVERNOR PLAN

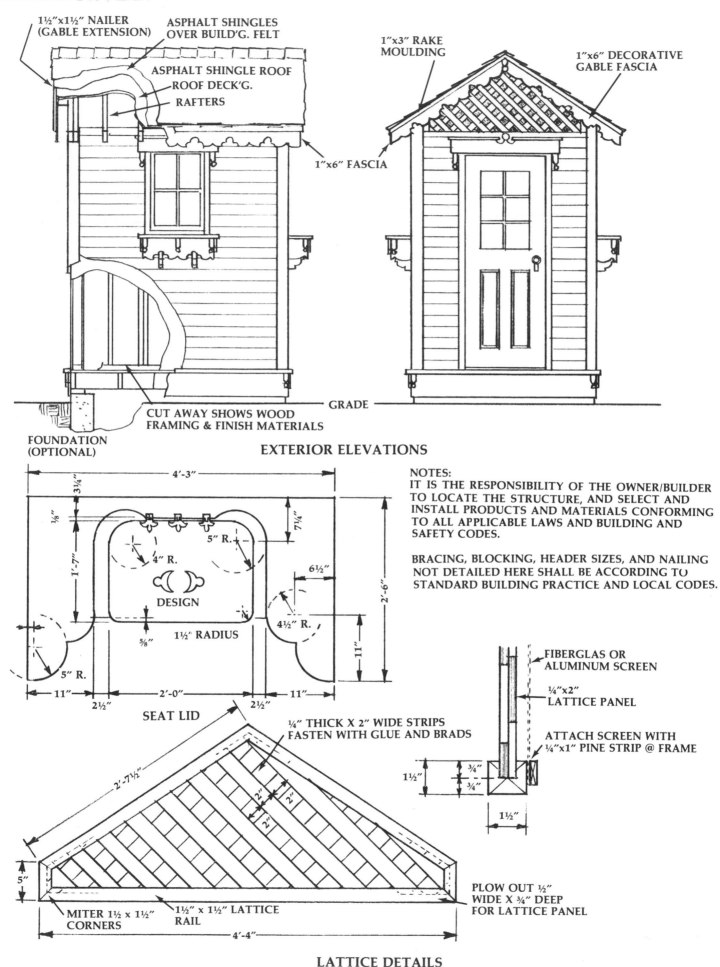

**1½"x1½" NAILER (GABLE EXTENSION)**

**ASPHALT SHINGLES OVER BUILD'G. FELT**

**ASPHALT SHINGLE ROOF**
**ROOF DECK'G.**
**RAFTERS**

**1"x3" RAKE MOULDING**

**1"x6" DECORATIVE GABLE FASCIA**

**1"x6" FASCIA**

**GRADE**

**CUT AWAY SHOWS WOOD FRAMING & FINISH MATERIALS**

**FOUNDATION (OPTIONAL)**

## EXTERIOR ELEVATIONS

4'-3"
3¼"
⅛"
1'-7"
5" R.
4" R.
5" R.
11"
2½"
2'-0"
2½"
11"
⅝"
1½' RADIUS
DESIGN
7¼"
6½"
4½" R.
2'-6"
11"

**SEAT LID**

NOTES:
IT IS THE RESPONSIBILITY OF THE OWNER/BUILDER TO LOCATE THE STRUCTURE, AND SELECT AND INSTALL PRODUCTS AND MATERIALS CONFORMING TO ALL APPLICABLE LAWS AND BUILDING AND SAFETY CODES.

BRACING, BLOCKING, HEADER SIZES, AND NAILING NOT DETAILED HERE SHALL BE ACCORDING TO STANDARD BUILDING PRACTICE AND LOCAL CODES.

**FIBERGLAS OR ALUMINUM SCREEN**

**¼"x2" LATTICE PANEL**

**ATTACH SCREEN WITH ¼"x1" PINE STRIP @ FRAME**

1½"
¾"
¾"
1½"

**¼" THICK X 2" WIDE STRIPS FASTEN WITH GLUE AND BRADS**

2'-7½"
2"
2"
2"
5"

**PLOW OUT ½" WIDE X ¾" DEEP FOR LATTICE PANEL**

**MITER 1½ x 1½ CORNERS**

**1½" x 1½" LATTICE RAIL**

4'-4"

## LATTICE DETAILS

74

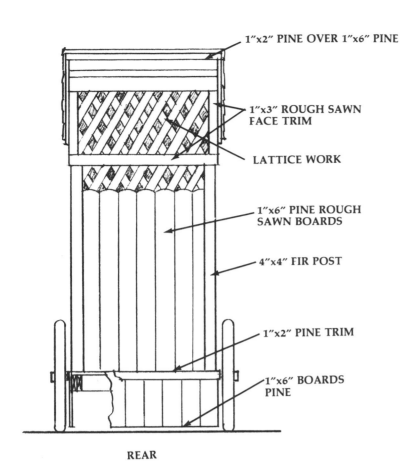

WOOD SHINGLE ROOF

1"x2" PINE OVER 1"x6" PINE

1"x3" ROUGH SAWN FACE TRIM

LATTICE WORK

1"x6" PINE ROUGH SAWN BOARDS

4"x4" FIR POST

1"x2" PINE TRIM

1"x6" BOARDS PINE

REAR

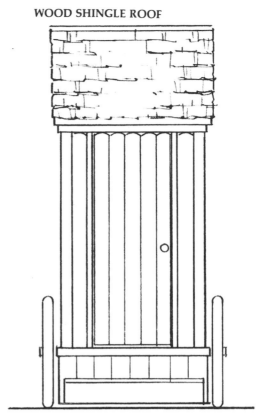

FRONT

CUTAWAY SHOWS FINISH AND CONSTRUCTION MAT'LS

USE WHEELCHAIR WHEELS (LESS HAND-RING) OR BICYCLE WHEELS AVAILABLE AT LOCAL BIKE SHOPS.
24" - 26" DIA.

STEP

GRADE

SIDE

NOTES:

*IT IS THE RESPONSIBILITY OF THE OWNER/ BUILDER TO SELECT AND INSTALL PRODUCTS AND MATERIALS CONFORMING TO ALL AP-PLICABLE LAWS AND BUILDING & SAFETY CODES.

*IT IS ALSO THE RESPONSIBILITY OF THE OWNER/BUILDER TO LOCATE THE STRUCTURE IN PLACES (IF MOBILE) CONSISTANT WITH LOCAL & STATE LAWS & CODES AND TO CON-STRUCT A TEMPORARY PIT CONFORMING TO SUCH LAWS & CODES.

*CONSTRUCTION METHODS NOT DETAILED HERE (BRACING, BLOCKING, HEADER SIZES, NAILING, ETC.) SHALL BE ACCORDING TO STANDARD BUILDING PRACTICE & LOCAL CODES.

EXTERIOR ELEVATIONS

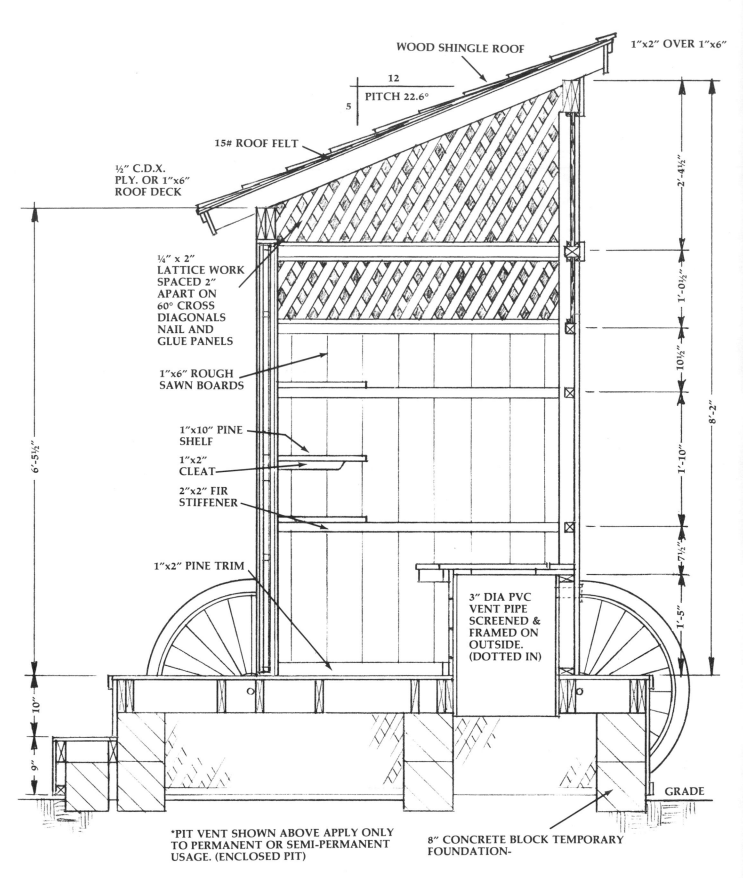

WOOD SHINGLE ROOF

1"x2" OVER 1"x6"

12
PITCH 22.6°
5

15# ROOF FELT

½" C.D.X.
PLY. OR 1"x6"
ROOF DECK

¼" x 2"
LATTICE WORK
SPACED 2"
APART ON
60° CROSS
DIAGONALS
NAIL AND
GLUE PANELS

1"x6" ROUGH
SAWN BOARDS

1"x10" PINE
SHELF

1"x2"
CLEAT

2"x2" FIR
STIFFENER

1"x2" PINE TRIM

3" DIA PVC
VENT PIPE
SCREENED &
FRAMED ON
OUTSIDE.
(DOTTED IN)

2'-4½"

1'-0½"

10½"

1'-10"

7½"

1'-5"

8'-2"

6'-5½"

10"

9"

GRADE

*PIT VENT SHOWN ABOVE APPLY ONLY
TO PERMANENT OR SEMI-PERMANENT
USAGE. (ENCLOSED PIT)

8" CONCRETE BLOCK TEMPORARY
FOUNDATION-

**SECTION**

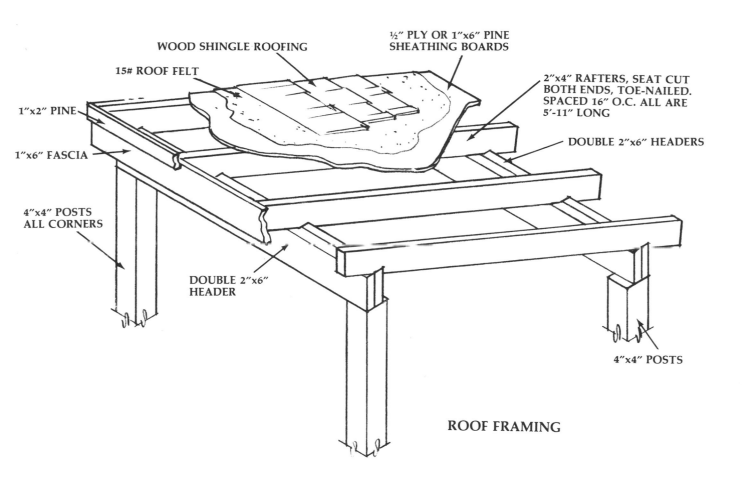

WOOD SHINGLE ROOFING

½" PLY OR 1"x6" PINE SHEATHING BOARDS

15# ROOF FELT

2"x4" RAFTERS, SEAT CUT BOTH ENDS, TOE-NAILED. SPACED 16" O.C. ALL ARE 5'-11" LONG

1"x2" PINE

1"x6" FASCIA

DOUBLE 2"x6" HEADERS

4"x4" POSTS ALL CORNERS

DOUBLE 2"x6" HEADER

4"x4" POSTS

**ROOF FRAMING**

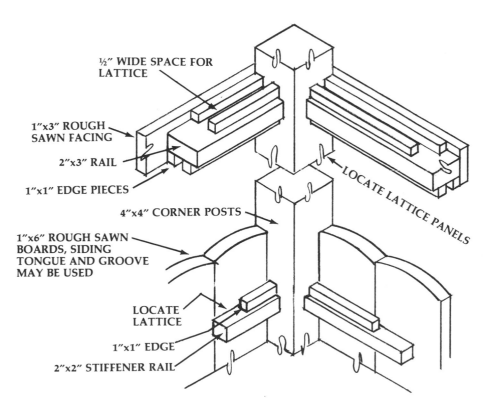

½" WIDE SPACE FOR LATTICE

1"x3" ROUGH SAWN FACING

2"x3" RAIL

1"x1" EDGE PIECES

LOCATE LATTICE PANELS

4"x4" CORNER POSTS

1"x6" ROUGH SAWN BOARDS, SIDING TONGUE AND GROOVE MAY BE USED

LOCATE LATTICE

1"x1" EDGE

2"x2" STIFFENER RAIL

**CORNER DETAIL**

# PRAIRIE SCHOONER PLAN

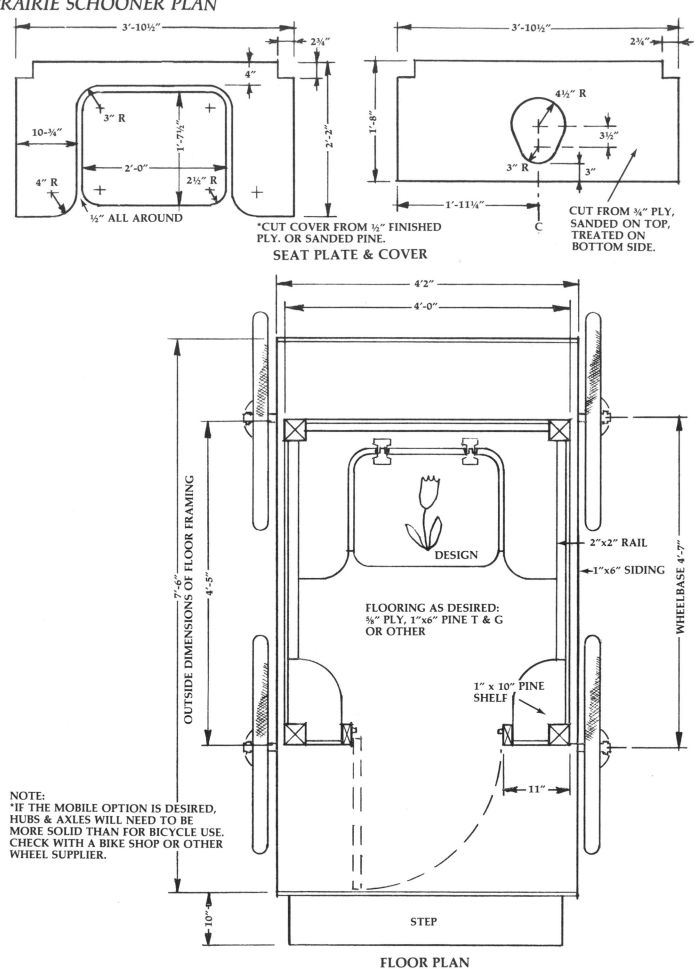

3'-10½"  2¾"  4"  2'-2"

3" R

10-¾"  1'-7½"

2'-0"  2½" R

4" R  ½" ALL AROUND

*CUT COVER FROM ½" FINISHED PLY. OR SANDED PINE.

**SEAT PLATE & COVER**

3'-10½"  2¾"

1'-8"

4½" R  3½"

3" R  3"

1'-11¼"  C

CUT FROM ¾" PLY, SANDED ON TOP, TREATED ON BOTTOM SIDE.

4'2"

4'-0"

OUTSIDE DIMENSIONS OF FLOOR FRAMING

7'-6"  4'-5"

2"x2" RAIL

1"x6" SIDING

WHEELBASE 4'-7"

DESIGN

FLOORING AS DESIRED:
⅝" PLY, 1"x6" PINE T & G
OR OTHER

1" x 10" PINE SHELF

11"

NOTE:
*IF THE MOBILE OPTION IS DESIRED, HUBS & AXLES WILL NEED TO BE MORE SOLID THAN FOR BICYCLE USE. CHECK WITH A BIKE SHOP OR OTHER WHEEL SUPPLIER.

10"

STEP

**FLOOR PLAN**

B. FORM UP 2" x 4" s PER SIZE REQUIREMENTS. FOR POURING CONCRETE SILL RING (FORM & POUR CAP FLOOR SIMILARLY PER SIZE).

C. ADD WIRE MESH REINFORCING BARS TO FORM. RAISE TO CENTER OF FINISHED CONC. THICKNESS FOR PROPER ADVANTAGE. YOU MAY FORM UP THE RISER, AND POUR AT THE SAME TIME.

D. POUR CONCRETE (5½ SACK MIX, ¾"Ø AGGREGATE) READY MIX.

E. USE THE SILL RING AT GROUND LEVEL AS A CONTINUOUS SUPPORT FOR THE FLOOR SLAB. INSERT EYEBOLTS IN WET CONCRETE (USE A STRETCHED STRING GUIDE) FOR LOCATING AND ANCHORING SLAB FLOOR.

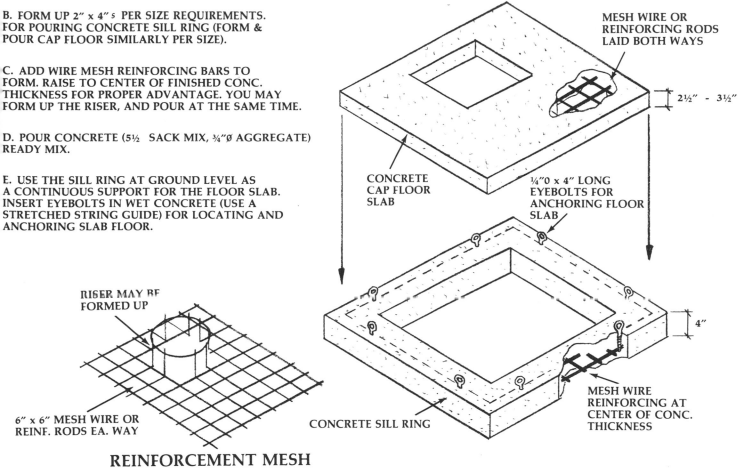

MESH WIRE OR REINFORCING RODS LAID BOTH WAYS

2½" - 3½"

CONCRETE CAP FLOOR SLAB

¼"Ø x 4" LONG EYEBOLTS FOR ANCHORING FLOOR SLAB

4"

MESH WIRE REINFORCING AT CENTER OF CONC. THICKNESS

CONCRETE SILL RING

RISER MAY BE FORMED UP

6" x 6" MESH WIRE OR REINF. RODS EA. WAY

**REINFORCEMENT MESH**

**SLAB CONSTRUCTION SEQUENCE**

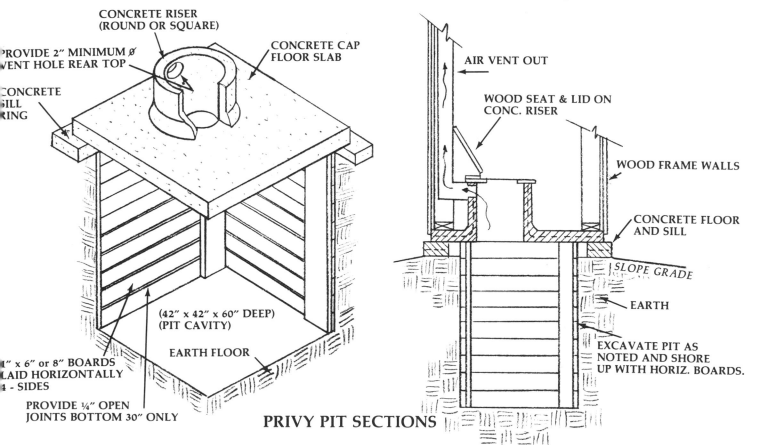

CONCRETE RISER (ROUND OR SQUARE)

CONCRETE CAP FLOOR SLAB

PROVIDE 2" MINIMUM Ø VENT HOLE REAR TOP

CONCRETE SILL RING

AIR VENT OUT

WOOD SEAT & LID ON CONC. RISER

WOOD FRAME WALLS

CONCRETE FLOOR AND SILL

SLOPE GRADE

(42" x 42" x 60" DEEP) (PIT CAVITY)

EARTH FLOOR

EARTH

EXCAVATE PIT AS NOTED AND SHORE UP WITH HORIZ. BOARDS.

1" x 6" or 8" BOARDS LAID HORIZONTALLY 4 - SIDES

PROVIDE ¼" OPEN JOINTS BOTTOM 30" ONLY

**PRIVY PIT SECTIONS**

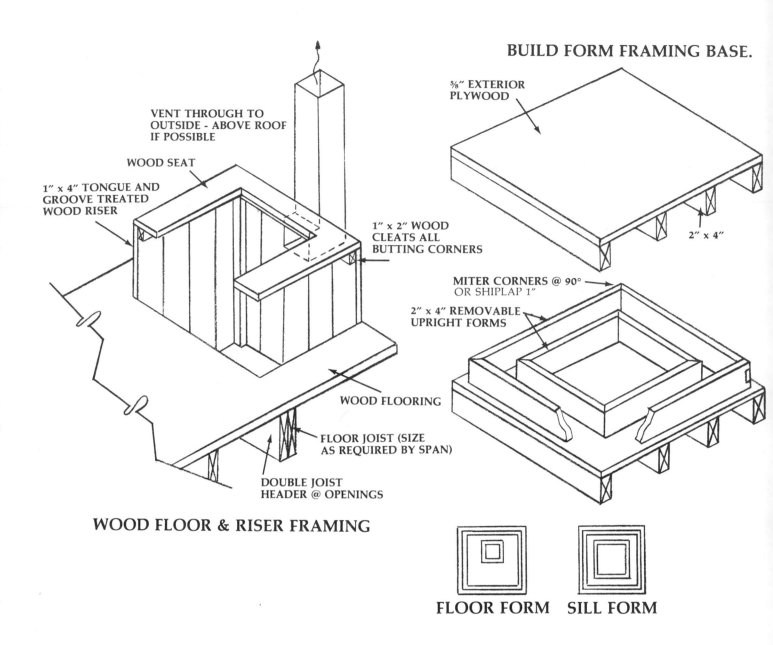

BUILD FORM FRAMING BASE.

⅝" EXTERIOR PLYWOOD

2" x 4"

VENT THROUGH TO OUTSIDE - ABOVE ROOF IF POSSIBLE

WOOD SEAT

1" x 4" TONGUE AND GROOVE TREATED WOOD RISER

1" x 2" WOOD CLEATS ALL BUTTING CORNERS

MITER CORNERS @ 90° OR SHIPLAP 1"

2" x 4" REMOVABLE UPRIGHT FORMS

WOOD FLOORING

FLOOR JOIST (SIZE AS REQUIRED BY SPAN)

DOUBLE JOIST HEADER @ OPENINGS

## WOOD FLOOR & RISER FRAMING

FLOOR FORM     SILL FORM

NOTE:
USE THESE PLANS AS A GENERAL GUIDE. AS WITH ALL MAJOR PROJECTS, RESEARCH THOROUGHLY AND STUDY THE CODES.

# INTERIOR SUGGESTIONS

We have shown, on the following pages, a few of the most popular uses that we have found for some of our Privies. General construction notes, dimensions, and designs are given to enable you to size the idea to your particular building or wall dimensions. While some of our buildings may be more appropriate for one thing than another, all of them can be used for any purpose and their use is only limited by your imagination.

In order to stimulate that imagination, we have included throughout the book additional ideas, such as puppet theatre, gym equipment, railroad track on the floor, etc.

Of course, for those people who have the need, we don't want to overlook these buildings as working Privies. Or, if you are just looking for decorating ideas for your bathroom or Privy, maybe you can find some good ideas on the accessories and interior pages.

We do not make or sell any of the items on these pages however. They are only ideas for you to create from.

*indoor shutters • plant shelf*

# SAUNA

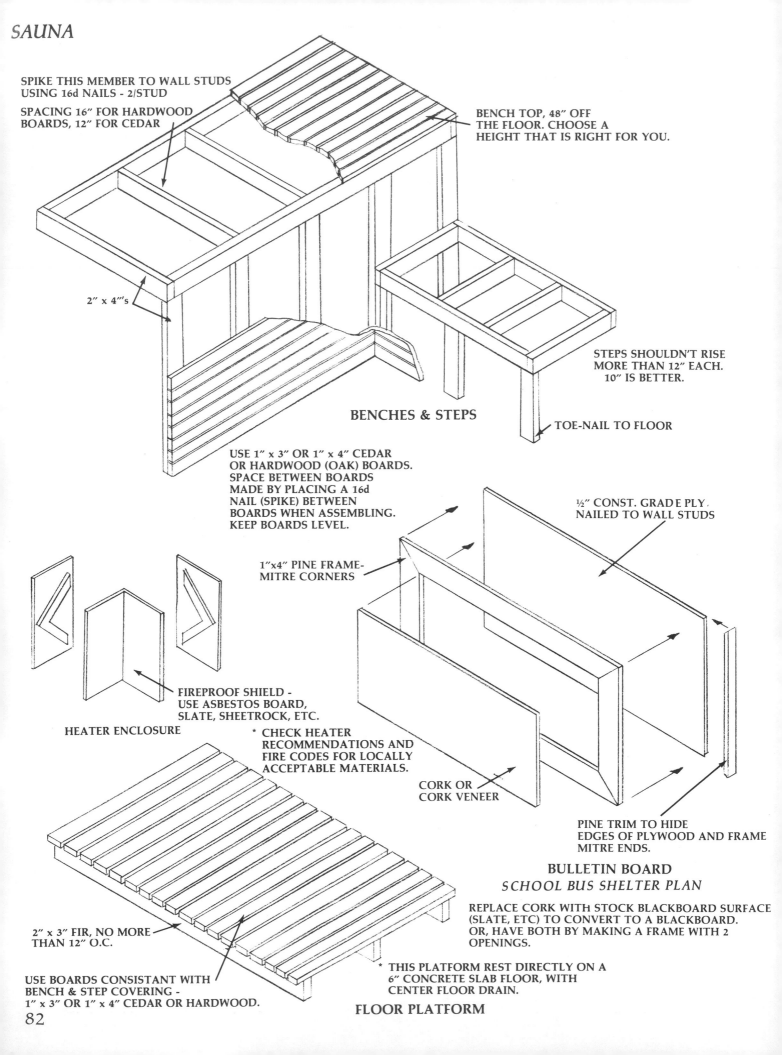

SPIKE THIS MEMBER TO WALL STUDS USING 16d NAILS - 2/STUD

SPACING 16" FOR HARDWOOD BOARDS, 12" FOR CEDAR

2" x 4"'s

BENCH TOP, 48" OFF THE FLOOR. CHOOSE A HEIGHT THAT IS RIGHT FOR YOU.

STEPS SHOULDN'T RISE MORE THAN 12" EACH. 10" IS BETTER.

TOE-NAIL TO FLOOR

**BENCHES & STEPS**

USE 1" x 3" OR 1" x 4" CEDAR OR HARDWOOD (OAK) BOARDS. SPACE BETWEEN BOARDS MADE BY PLACING A 16d NAIL (SPIKE) BETWEEN BOARDS WHEN ASSEMBLING. KEEP BOARDS LEVEL.

FIREPROOF SHIELD - USE ASBESTOS BOARD, SLATE, SHEETROCK, ETC.

HEATER ENCLOSURE

* CHECK HEATER RECOMMENDATIONS AND FIRE CODES FOR LOCALLY ACCEPTABLE MATERIALS.

½" CONST. GRADE PLY, NAILED TO WALL STUDS

1"x4" PINE FRAME- MITRE CORNERS

CORK OR CORK VENEER

PINE TRIM TO HIDE EDGES OF PLYWOOD AND FRAME MITRE ENDS.

**BULLETIN BOARD**
*SCHOOL BUS SHELTER PLAN*

REPLACE CORK WITH STOCK BLACKBOARD SURFACE (SLATE, ETC) TO CONVERT TO A BLACKBOARD. OR, HAVE BOTH BY MAKING A FRAME WITH 2 OPENINGS.

2" x 3" FIR, NO MORE THAN 12" O.C.

USE BOARDS CONSISTANT WITH BENCH & STEP COVERING - 1" x 3" OR 1" x 4" CEDAR OR HARDWOOD.

* THIS PLATFORM REST DIRECTLY ON A 6" CONCRETE SLAB FLOOR, WITH CENTER FLOOR DRAIN.

**FLOOR PLATFORM**

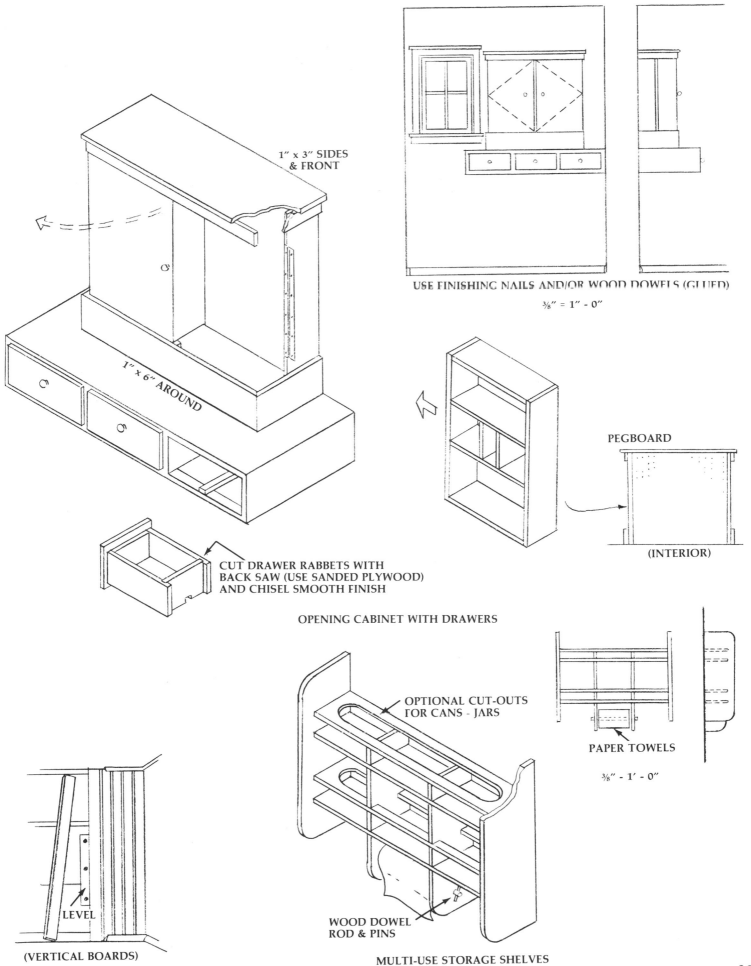

1" x 3" SIDES & FRONT

1" x 6" AROUND

USE FINISHING NAILS AND/OR WOOD DOWELS (GLUED)

$\frac{3}{8}'' = 1'' - 0''$

CUT DRAWER RABBETS WITH BACK SAW (USE SANDED PLYWOOD) AND CHISEL SMOOTH FINISH

OPENING CABINET WITH DRAWERS

PEGBOARD

(INTERIOR)

OPTIONAL CUT-OUTS FOR CANS - JARS

PAPER TOWELS

$\frac{3}{8}'' - 1' - 0''$

LEVEL

WOOD DOWEL ROD & PINS

(VERTICAL BOARDS)

MULTI-USE STORAGE SHELVES

# SCHOOL BUS SHELTER

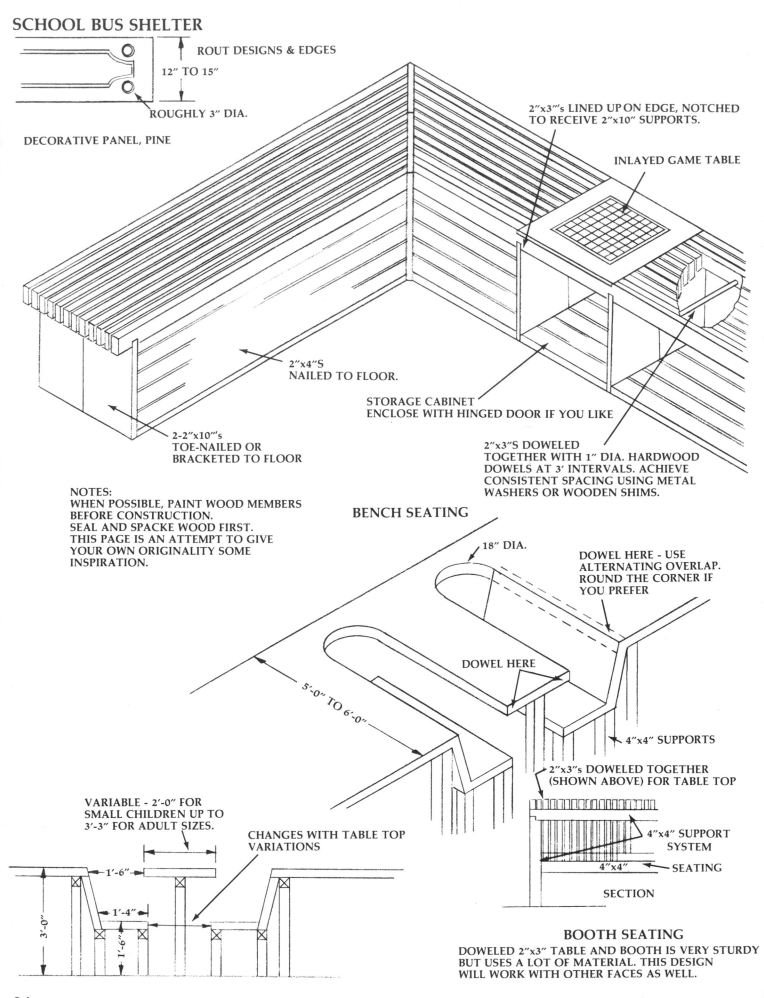

ROUT DESIGNS & EDGES

12" TO 15"

ROUGHLY 3" DIA.

DECORATIVE PANEL, PINE

2"x3"s LINED UP ON EDGE, NOTCHED
TO RECEIVE 2"x10" SUPPORTS.

INLAYED GAME TABLE

2"x4"S
NAILED TO FLOOR.

STORAGE CABINET
ENCLOSE WITH HINGED DOOR IF YOU LIKE

2-2"x10"'s
TOE-NAILED OR
BRACKETED TO FLOOR

2"x3"S DOWELED
TOGETHER WITH 1" DIA. HARDWOOD
DOWELS AT 3' INTERVALS. ACHIEVE
CONSISTENT SPACING USING METAL
WASHERS OR WOODEN SHIMS.

NOTES:
WHEN POSSIBLE, PAINT WOOD MEMBERS
BEFORE CONSTRUCTION.
SEAL AND SPACKE WOOD FIRST.
THIS PAGE IS AN ATTEMPT TO GIVE
YOUR OWN ORIGINALITY SOME
INSPIRATION.

## BENCH SEATING

18" DIA.

DOWEL HERE - USE
ALTERNATING OVERLAP.
ROUND THE CORNER IF
YOU PREFER

DOWEL HERE

5'-0" TO 6'-0"

4"x4" SUPPORTS

2"x3"s DOWELED TOGETHER
(SHOWN ABOVE) FOR TABLE TOP

VARIABLE - 2'-0" FOR
SMALL CHILDREN UP TO
3'-3" FOR ADULT SIZES.

CHANGES WITH TABLE TOP
VARIATIONS

1'-6"

3'-0"

1'-4"

1'-6"

4"x4" SUPPORT
SYSTEM

4"x4" — SEATING

SECTION

## BOOTH SEATING

DOWELED 2"x3" TABLE AND BOOTH IS VERY STURDY
BUT USES A LOT OF MATERIAL. THIS DESIGN
WILL WORK WITH OTHER FACES AS WELL.

84

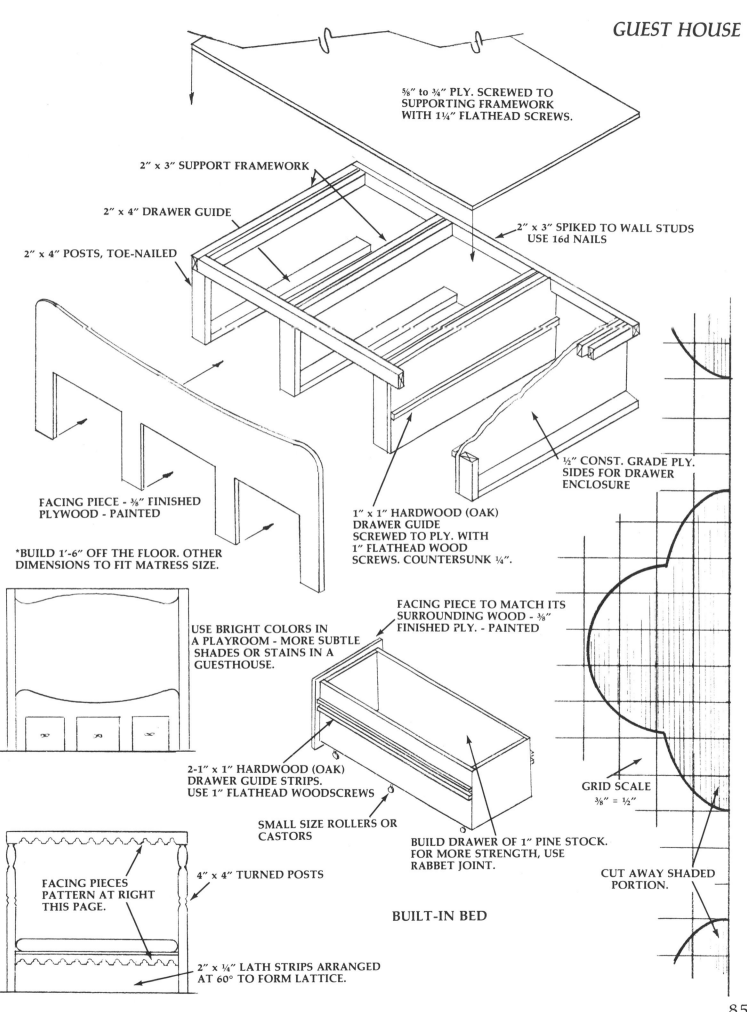

⅝" to ¾" PLY. SCREWED TO
SUPPORTING FRAMEWORK
WITH 1¼" FLATHEAD SCREWS.

2" x 3" SUPPORT FRAMEWORK

2" x 4" DRAWER GUIDE

2" x 4" POSTS, TOE-NAILED

2" x 3" SPIKED TO WALL STUDS
USE 16d NAILS

FACING PIECE - ⅜" FINISHED
PLYWOOD - PAINTED

½" CONST. GRADE PLY.
SIDES FOR DRAWER
ENCLOSURE

*BUILD 1'-6" OFF THE FLOOR. OTHER
DIMENSIONS TO FIT MATRESS SIZE.

1" x 1" HARDWOOD (OAK)
DRAWER GUIDE
SCREWED TO PLY. WITH
1" FLATHEAD WOOD
SCREWS. COUNTERSUNK ¼".

FACING PIECE TO MATCH ITS
SURROUNDING WOOD - ⅜"
FINISHED PLY. - PAINTED

USE BRIGHT COLORS IN
A PLAYROOM - MORE SUBTLE
SHADES OR STAINS IN A
GUESTHOUSE.

2-1" x 1" HARDWOOD (OAK)
DRAWER GUIDE STRIPS.
USE 1" FLATHEAD WOODSCREWS.

SMALL SIZE ROLLERS OR
CASTORS

BUILD DRAWER OF 1" PINE STOCK.
FOR MORE STRENGTH, USE
RABBET JOINT.

GRID SCALE
⅜" = ½"

CUT AWAY SHADED
PORTION.

FACING PIECES
PATTERN AT RIGHT
THIS PAGE.

4" x 4" TURNED POSTS

2" x ¼" LATH STRIPS ARRANGED
AT 60° TO FORM LATTICE.

**BUILT-IN BED**

# PLAYHOUSE

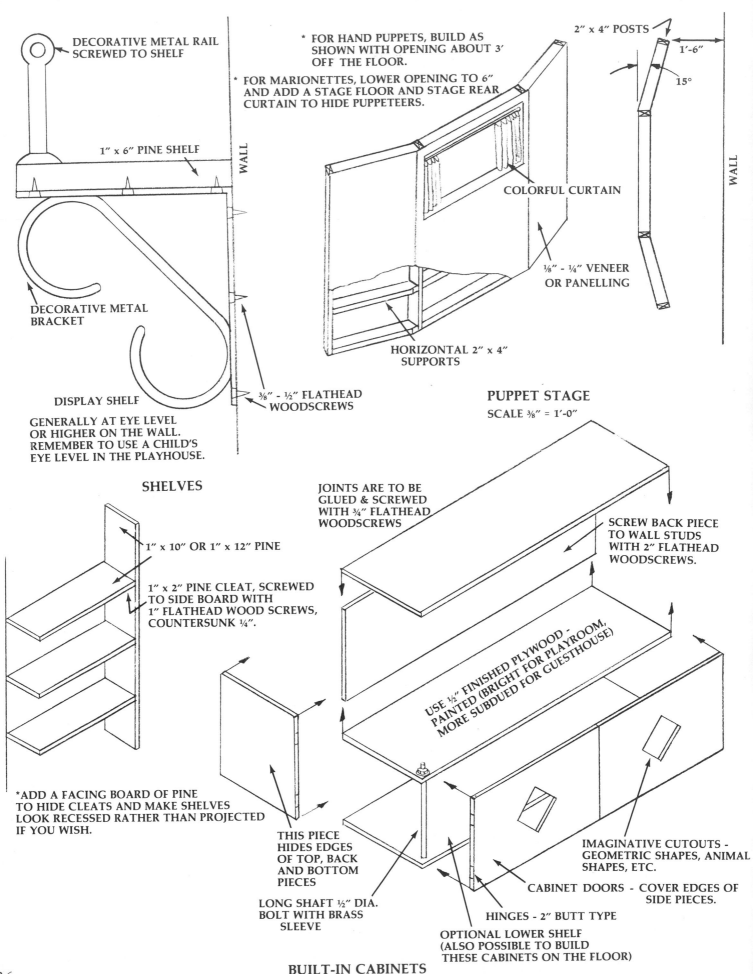

DECORATIVE METAL RAIL SCREWED TO SHELF

1" x 6" PINE SHELF

WALL

DECORATIVE METAL BRACKET

DISPLAY SHELF

GENERALLY AT EYE LEVEL OR HIGHER ON THE WALL. REMEMBER TO USE A CHILD'S EYE LEVEL IN THE PLAYHOUSE.

3/8" - 1/2" FLATHEAD WOODSCREWS

* FOR HAND PUPPETS, BUILD AS SHOWN WITH OPENING ABOUT 3' OFF THE FLOOR.

* FOR MARIONETTES, LOWER OPENING TO 6" AND ADD A STAGE FLOOR AND STAGE REAR CURTAIN TO HIDE PUPPETEERS.

COLORFUL CURTAIN

1/8" - 1/4" VENEER OR PANELLING

HORIZONTAL 2" x 4" SUPPORTS

2" x 4" POSTS

1'-6"

15°

WALL

PUPPET STAGE
SCALE 3/8" = 1'-0"

## SHELVES

1" x 10" OR 1" x 12" PINE

1" x 2" PINE CLEAT, SCREWED TO SIDE BOARD WITH 1" FLATHEAD WOOD SCREWS, COUNTERSUNK 1/4".

*ADD A FACING BOARD OF PINE TO HIDE CLEATS AND MAKE SHELVES LOOK RECESSED RATHER THAN PROJECTED IF YOU WISH.

JOINTS ARE TO BE GLUED & SCREWED WITH 3/4" FLATHEAD WOODSCREWS

SCREW BACK PIECE TO WALL STUDS WITH 2" FLATHEAD WOODSCREWS.

USE 1/2" FINISHED PLYWOOD - PAINTED (BRIGHT FOR PLAYROOM, MORE SUBDUED FOR GUESTHOUSE)

THIS PIECE HIDES EDGES OF TOP, BACK AND BOTTOM PIECES

LONG SHAFT 1/2" DIA. BOLT WITH BRASS SLEEVE

IMAGINATIVE CUTOUTS - GEOMETRIC SHAPES, ANIMAL SHAPES, ETC.

CABINET DOORS - COVER EDGES OF SIDE PIECES.

HINGES - 2" BUTT TYPE

OPTIONAL LOWER SHELF (ALSO POSSIBLE TO BUILD THESE CABINETS ON THE FLOOR)

## BUILT-IN CABINETS

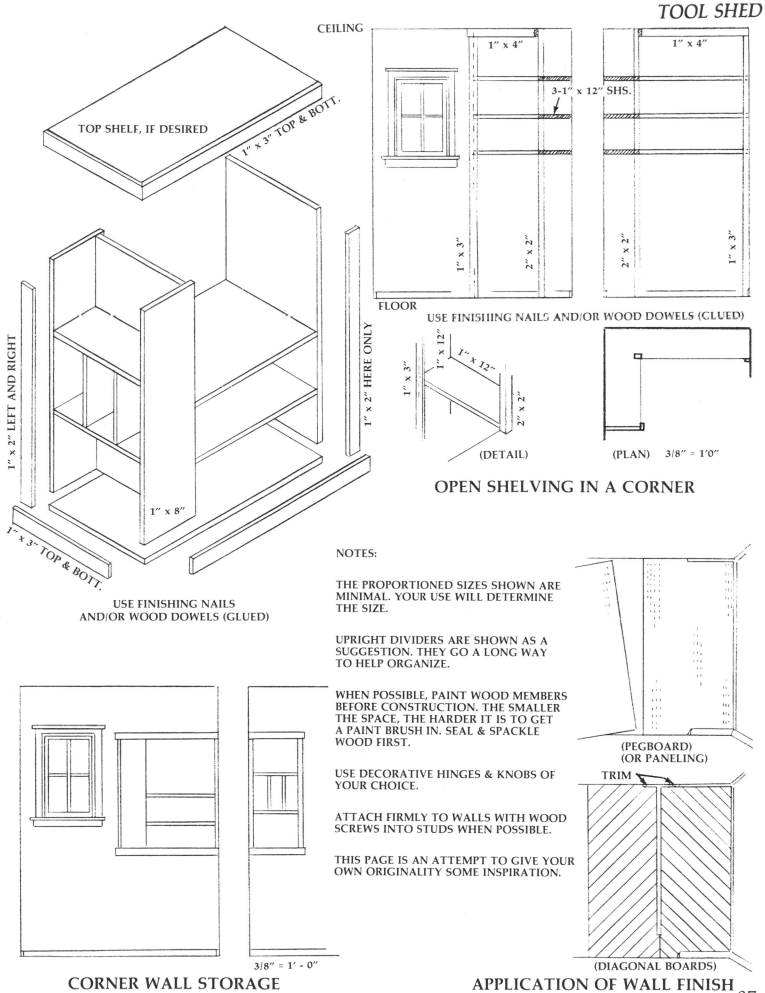

TOP SHELF, IF DESIRED

1" x 3" TOP & BOTT.

1" x 2" LEFT AND RIGHT

1" x 3" TOP & BOTT.

1" x 8"

USE FINISHING NAILS
AND/OR WOOD DOWELS (GLUED)

CEILING

1" x 4"

3-1" x 12" SHS.

1" x 3"

2" x 2"

FLOOR

1" x 4"

2" x 2"

1" x 3"

1" x 2" HERE ONLY

USE FINISHING NAILS AND/OR WOOD DOWELS (GLUED)

1" x 3"

1" x 12"

1" x 12"

2" x 2"

(DETAIL)

(PLAN)    3/8" = 1'0"

## OPEN SHELVING IN A CORNER

NOTES:

THE PROPORTIONED SIZES SHOWN ARE MINIMAL. YOUR USE WILL DETERMINE THE SIZE.

UPRIGHT DIVIDERS ARE SHOWN AS A SUGGESTION. THEY GO A LONG WAY TO HELP ORGANIZE.

WHEN POSSIBLE, PAINT WOOD MEMBERS BEFORE CONSTRUCTION. THE SMALLER THE SPACE, THE HARDER IT IS TO GET A PAINT BRUSH IN. SEAL & SPACKLE WOOD FIRST.

USE DECORATIVE HINGES & KNOBS OF YOUR CHOICE.

ATTACH FIRMLY TO WALLS WITH WOOD SCREWS INTO STUDS WHEN POSSIBLE.

THIS PAGE IS AN ATTEMPT TO GIVE YOUR OWN ORIGINALITY SOME INSPIRATION.

(PEGBOARD)
(OR PANELING)

TRIM

(DIAGONAL BOARDS)

3/8" = 1' - 0"

## CORNER WALL STORAGE

## APPLICATION OF WALL FINISH

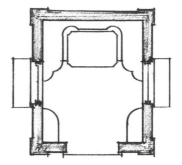

**GOVERNOR**
6'-0" x 5'-0" x 9'-9" H.

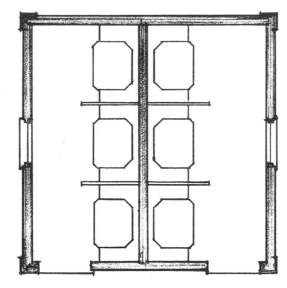

**ROSE GARDEN**
10'-8" x 10'-8" x 14'-4" H.

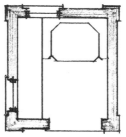

**GREENHOUSE**
5'-0" x 4'-6" x 10'-6" H.

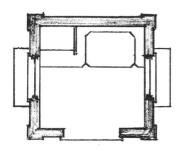

**OZARK**
5'-0" x 4'-6" x 10'-0" H.

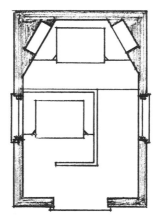

**ORIENTAL**
8'-0" x 5'-4" x 9'-8" H.

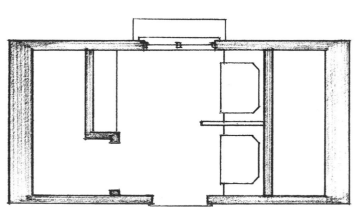

**CHALET**
14'-0" x 6'-8" x 12'-9" H.

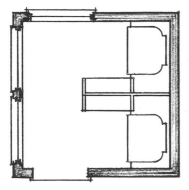

**GLAS HAUS**
7'-0" x 7'-0" x 10'-4" H.

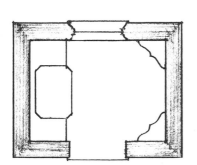

**VIKING**
7'-0" x 5'-8" x 9'-0" H.

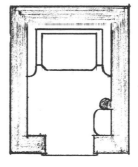

**NORTHERNAIRE**
6'-0" x 4'-8" x 10'-4" H.

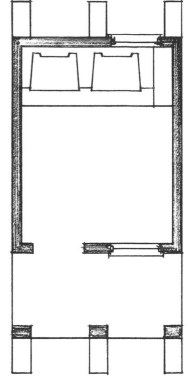

**SHANTY**
15'-6" x 7'-0" x 11'-4" H.

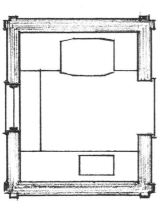

**PIONEER**
7'-4" x 6'-0" x 10'-6" H.

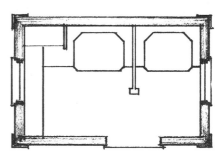

**DEW DROP INN**
8'-0" x 5'-4" x 10'-7" H.

# FLOOR PLANS

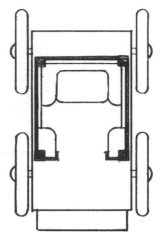

**PRAIRIE SCHOONER**
7'-6" x 4'-2" x 10'-7" H.

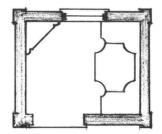

**SPRINGFIELD**
5'-6" x 4'-6" x 10'-6" H.

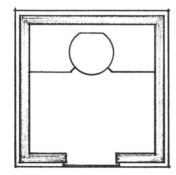

**LIGHT HOUSE**
6'-5" x 6'-5" x 13'-4" H.

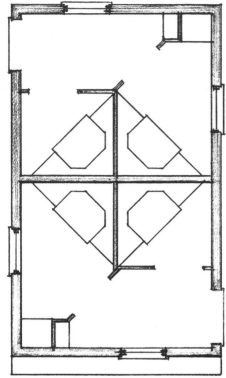

**BUNKHOUSE**
14'-8" x 8'-8" x 10'-4" H.

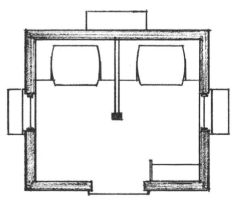

**CANTINA**
7'-8" x 6'-4" x 10'-0" H.

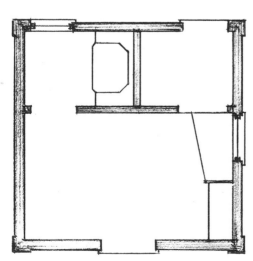

**MARBLEHEAD**
10'-0" x 10'-0" x 11'-0" H.

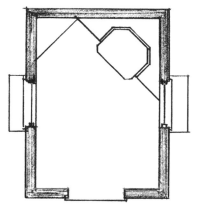

**OLDE BAILEY**
8'-0" x 6'-0" x 10'-5" H.

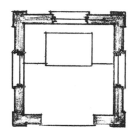

**YACHT CLUB**
4'-6" x 4'-6" x 11'-0" H.

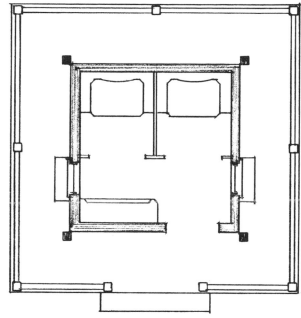

**KNOB HILL**
12'-0" x 12'-0" x 13'-5" H.

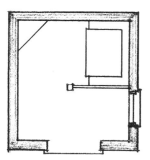

**THE PROVERBIAL BRICK HOUSE**
6'-0" x 5'-4" x 10'-9" H.

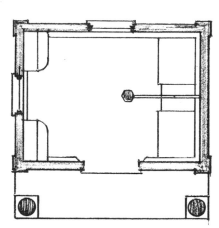

**ROMAN BATH**
8'-0" x 8'-0" x 10'-8" H.

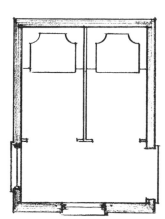

**DEPOT**
8'-0" x 6'-0" x 11'-3" H.

# PLAN PRICE LIST

Page   7. PRAIRIE SCHOONER ........................................................ 14.95

             PRAIRIE SCHOONER POSTER - 17x22 ................................ 3.50

       9. GREENHOUSE ................................................................. 12.95

    11. GOVERNOR .................................................................... 14.95

    13. KNOB HILL ..................................................................... 18.95

    15. ORIENTAL ...................................................................... 14.95

    17. SHANTY ......................................................................... 14.95

    19. OZARK ........................................................................... 12.95

    21. CAN-TINA ...................................................................... 14.95

    23. GLAS HAUS ................................................................... 12.95

    25. DEW DROP INN ............................................................. 14.95

    27. ROSE GARDEN ............................................................. 12.95

    29. DEPOT ........................................................................... 14.95

    31. TEE PEE ......................................................................... 12.95

    33. THE VIKING ................................................................... 14.95

    35. THE ROMAN BATH ........................................................ 18.95

    37. PIONEER ........................................................................ 12.95

    39. CHALET .......................................................................... 14.95

    41. SPRINGFIELD ................................................................ 12.95

    43. OLDE BAILEY ................................................................ 12.95

    45. PROVERBIAL BRICK HOUSE ........................................ 12.95

    47. YACHT CLUB ................................................................. 12.95

    51. MARBLEHEAD ............................................................... 14.95

    53. BUNK HOUSE ................................................................ 14.95

    55. LIGHT HOUSE ............................................................... 14.95

Every plan includes special design layouts for a sauna, a playhouse, a school bus shelter, a guest house, and a tool shed. Material lists for mini-plans furnished upon request.

SUN DESIGNS
P.O. Box 206
Delafield, WI 53018